Happiness on a Shoestring

Finding Joy in Trying Times

Bonnie Cobb Skinner

A Lady Among Ladies

I am delighted to dedicate this book to my
dear friend and mentor, Florence Littauer. Her
bright spirit and constant encouragement continue
to uplift me every day. Florence, thank you for
giving me the freedom to be just the way God
made me, a Sanguine-Choleric!

Special Thanks

With love and appreciation to my
friends and family for your continued love
and encouragement, and especially to
my husband, Jack.

ISBN-13: 978-0-615-33589-6

HAPPINESS ON A SHOESTRING
Finding Joy in Trying Times

OUR LIVES ARE LIKE A SHOESTRING

Straightened out,
the shoestring is simple and ready to take on the world.
If the shoestring becomes knotted and tangled,
It takes on a different look and meaning.
If we take good care of the shoestring, it will last indefinitely.
If we let mud, dirt, and grime collect,
The chances of its wearing out quickly are increased.
If we tie the shoestring in tight, hard knots,
the threads will wear thin and it will eventually break.

So it is with life ~ if we live a good clean life,
Keeping things in perspective, we can be happy.
If we set good examples and keep the weeds out of our lives,
we can be strong.
If we allow our lives to become tangled, we will find ourselves
struggling to get free from the knots that bind us.
If we avoid pitfalls, we can achieve our maximum potential,
regardless of our circumstances.

If we live balanced lives in the areas of mind, body and soul,
we can gain the inner peace and happiness we seek.
I am the master of my fate and the captain of my soul,
And, YOU can be, too!

That's what "Happiness On A Shoestring" is all about!

- Bonnie Skinner, 1988

*"And let us consider how we may spur one another
on toward love and good deeds."*
~ Hebrews 10:24

Table of Contents

Table of Contents

1

Living Life
on a Shoestring

Some people are born with a silver spoon in their mouth ~ I had a shoestring in mine! I was born on February 18, 1931, during the Great Depression. At that time, my parents were living in the home of my grandparents in Marshall County, Alabama. My grandparents were considering a permanent move to nearby Albertville; however, they eventually decided to return to their homestead. It was then that my parents bought their own home in the same general area. My first childhood memories center around that little house "down the road". A few years later, we moved up the

Bonnie's
Birthplace

highway to the Freeman's Chapel community in DeKalb County. It was there where I spent most of my childhood years.

My earliest recollection at about age two is of sitting on my mother's lap by the pot belly stove at Freeman's Chapel. I remember gazing up at the rafters in the unfinished ceiling while being passed from one woman to another to keep me occupied while my parents were both on the church stage participating in the music. I heard someone commenting on my curly hair but I just wanted my mother.

As a very young child, I remember visiting my mother's relatives in Florida. During that trip, my dad placed me in a small boxcar on a miniature train ride and as it went in a big circle, I wondered why everyone was smiling because I was so scared! Mother often mentioned putting my baby brother's feet in the Gulf of Mexico on that trip when he was only six weeks old. Later, I asked her if I waded in the water as well, she curtly replied, "I just don't remember!" We children learned to take the hard knocks right along with the positive ones.

We began our lives at an interesting time when there was no running water or electricity in our houses. We had oil lamps for light at night time. Providing wood for heating the houses in the winter and fires in the kitchen stoves was a major concern for the fathers. We drew water from a well located underneath our back porch. There was a cedar bucket and dipper nearby and if we became thirsty, we simply drank a dipper of water. Several years ago, I stopped by that little house and asked if I might draw a pail of water and get a cool drink, which I did, and it was just as I remembered!

As a four year old, I recall standing by my mother in front of our house as we watched a funeral procession crossing over a nearby hill. She said it was for my great-grandfather, Samuel Houston Cobb, and they were en route to Concord Church for his burial. Mother had tears in her eyes and I wondered why.

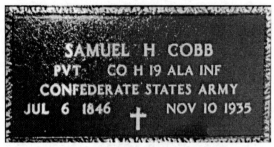

SAMUEL H COBB
PVT   CO H 19 ALA INF
CONFEDERATE STATES ARMY
JUL 6 1846 + NOV 10 1935

Plaque of Bonnie's Great-Grandad

Since mother's relatives lived in Tampa, Florida, we visited them again when I was age six. I remember drinking milk poured from a glass bottle which the milkman had delivered to my aunt's front door. Being from the country, I was amazed all of this was accomplished without a cow!

Other childhood memories include riding my little brother's tricycle through our house and hiding behind a burgundy brocade curtain handed down from a past generation. In our pasture, we played on a large rock resembling a sheep, and we kept our milk chilled in a nearby cold running spring until we bought our first ice box. Mother starkly threatened, "You'd better not go near that spring! There's snappin' turtles out there!" These are just some highlights of our life back in the 1930's.

My first memory of any kind of refrigeration in our kitchen was the "ice box". On top of our ice box was a compartment which held a large block of ice to chill the food inside. Occasionally, the melting ice dripped onto the floor and mother would get furious, questioning the worth of it, even though Daddy had been so proud that he got it for her. I remember when we bought our first electric refrigerator. It was a thrill to think the light would be shining every time the door was opened.

I shared some of these memories with my cousin, Mel Tillis, and of course he has his own shoestring memories! He remembers the ice box his family had. His daddy bored a hole in the floor beneath the ice box and added a funnel to allow the overhead block of ice to drain underneath. He said, "Mama would let us put coffee grounds, corn meal and eggshells down there for our worm bed! The wet ground also helped pick up far away radio stations with the grounding rod! We had a copper rod stuck in that wet ground and could pick up the Grand Ole Opry ~ Wow! Those were the good ole days!" Thanks, Mel! That worm bed later provided fishing bait. I remember my Grandmother, Nettie Slaten (Mama), telling us about selling worms for bait from her back yard worm bed in Tampa, Florida. "There's money to be made!" Mama said!

I remember when our first home was wired for electricity. A cord dangled overhead with a single white shiny light bulb providing light. Still other events helped to mold my childhood. While a preschooler I noticed a picture in the Sunday magazine section of the newspaper which showed a little girl and boy playing in the sand with pails and shovels. I continued looking at the picture during the week which evidently made an impression on my dad. One day he came in with two pails and shovels for my little brother, Ken, and me! We spent many hours playing in the sand under our back porch, which seemed high off the ground at the time. When I revisited that little house, the back porch was only about three feet at its highest point from the ground.

Another fond memory at that young age was holding onto my dad's leg and looking up into his face. He had just returned from a long trip and I was so glad to see him. These reflections are the things which give children inner confidence. We learned to appreciate the things we had, which were quite meager up to this point in our lives ~ but, again, that was life back in the thirties.

While a very young girl, my dad bought me some red sandals at nearby Albertville, about five miles from our home. When he told me to try them on for sizing, I managed to squeeze my feet into them and vowed they fit just fine. He bought them, but within a short time, I had blisters on both feet, and that was the last time I saw the red sandals.

At about age seven or eight years, I received a winter coat which was bought at Dobson's Department Store in Albertville. There were always great buys at Dobson's because fire damaged and salvaged items were sold at discount prices. My coat was beige with a reversible brown velvet-lined detachable hood. Since I had always worn hand-me-downs, this was my first "store-bought" coat, and I felt very special when I wore it even though it smelled of smoke. I didn't complain because I feared my dad would return it to Albertville, as he did with the red sandals.

Walking up the sandy road to our grandparent's nearby home was a favorite thing to do. Grandmother

Cobb kept a neat, clean house and always had plenty of food underneath the table cloth in her kitchen. I especially enjoyed eating one of the baked sweet potatoes she usually kept in the overhead warmer of her kitchen stove, which was a great snack for children at that time. I liked to sit on the big stove wood box by the stove and kitchen window. This large wooden box with a lid contained wood used to heat that stove for cooking. One of my fondest memories of sitting on that wooden box was the day when one of my uncles, Breman, came up to me as I sat there and said, "Bonnie Jean, I will give you this orange if you will call me 'Uncle Breman.'" I promised him I would, but don't remember if I kept my promise! He was the youngest of Daddy's brothers and movie star handsome. He had a flair and drive for entertaining and possessed a great voice. He played the piano and accordion beautifully and was the leader of a band for quite some time. He yearned for a career in show business but was probably ahead of his time. Looking back, he could have become another Lawrence Welk with the proper guidance!

Later, when I was school age, I remember spending nights at my grandparent's house on many occasions. Once the lights were out, it was very dark in the guest bedroom. Over the mantel and fireplace, Grandmother had a large picture of a little boy and girl crossing a stream of water on a dangerous

looking bridge. An angel is hovering overhead and I always felt comfort in knowing that angel was in the picture. I would silently tell the little boy and girl in that picture, "Don't worry, the angel will take care of you!" That comforting thought also helped me go to sleep in that dark room. Today, I have a copy of that big picture in my home.

I have many fond memories of playing with cousins outside our grandparent's house; especially enjoying the fragrance of the lilac bushes as we played hide and seek around the porches which practically surrounded the house. I remember sitting on a large pile of picked cotton on our grandparent's front porch while visiting with my cousin, Peggy. My brother, Kenny, and I enjoyed "drawing" a pail of water from the back porch well and pouring it in the nearby cedar bucket. Every Christmas Grandmother decorated a huge holly tree with shiny red berries which stood in the large entry hall of their house.

Grandmother loved to tell the story of how she was trying to keep me pacified one day when I was about two years old. As she held me in her arms, she turned on the "Victrola" to distract me and a sacred harp song began playing. Evidentally, I didn't like it because she said I leaned over and spit on the cylindrical tube as it was going around! I remember that Victrola had a handle which had to be turned several times in order for the tube to operate since this was before electricity was available. This was a prelude to the 78 rpm records!

Our Grandad Cobb was often working in his garden, waiting to tease the grandchildren as they approached his house. He always had pleasant comments when we children were visiting. In a husky voice, he would growl, "What are you doin' in my yard!" I also remember Grandaddy saying, "What are you doin' on my back porch?!" He scared us but we really knew that he was joking. Many of the Cobb descendants are named for these loving grandparents, Nancy Jane and William David Cobb.

On laundry day, Grandmother heated two large iron pots of water in the back yard by burning sticks of wood underneath. To cool the ashes afterwards, she spread them out on the surrounding ground. On one visit, I did not realize the ashes were still very hot and I ran through those hot coals barefooted burning both feet. While I was sobbing, Grandmother rubbed salve on my feet. My Grandad made some little crutches for me. At this point, I began to daydream about how wonderful it must be to live in the city.

Grandmother Cobb always seemed to have things under control and I admired her very much. She always made time for us. I remember one day she sat in her favorite chair by the fire-place and let me comb her long grey hair ~ a lovely memory for me especially, because I was born in that room! What a blessing to have grandparents who give love and time to their grandchildren.

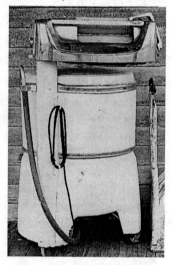

When our dad brought home our first wringer-type washing machine, the entire family stayed up late that night washing every dirty garment we could find. It was an amazing sight to watch the wet clothes go through the automatic wringer and come out totally smashed! Mother warned, "Don't put your hands in there ~ that wringer will break your arm!"

As the third daughter, I wore many hand-me-down dresses. Happiness on a Shoestring came for me when I grew too tall to receive anymore slightly worn dresses from my two older sisters! Mother used to remind me to stand still while she pinned my waist tighter with a safety pin on a too-big skirt. I remember having to basically "hold" a skirt in place on occasion.

In our densely populated rural area, the primary sources of income were cotton, corn and sorghum cane. Good stock, hard work, pride, optimism, ambition, and an innate sense of direction gave both my parents the necessary drive to forge ahead and achieve their dreams and goals. They had great vision and were pioneers of their time.

During this time all families struggled to make ends meet and ours was no exception. We learned the value of a dollar at an early age and I'm glad to say those principles have stayed with me for a lifetime. I saw how my parents made use of everything they owned, throwing away very little. Theirs was an uphill climb, but they made it gracefully and did it their way. I learned to be happy living on a shoestring and I'm happy to share some of my stories with you. This book didn't just happen ~ I lived it!

In 1938, when my brother, Ken, was five and I was seven years old, our parents took us to Tampa, Florida, for a visit with Mother's relatives. Our two older sisters stayed behind with the Alabama grandparents.

Always economizing, we drove directly to Tampa from north Alabama, stopping only for gasoline to include rest stops. We ate crackers, cheese, and oranges along the way. Daddy had little use for motels or "other extravagancies" even though this was before motels actually became popular for travelers. He considered those stops a waste of time and money. So, we had a very long, boring drive with short breaks.

For our trip from north Alabama to Tampa, Daddy placed an empty nail keg in front of Mother's knees in our Ford pickup truck. This was to be the seat for five year old Ken during the long trip. I was to sit quietly between my parents. My mother kept us in line but my dad was definitely head of the house. He repeatedly told my little brother to sit still and stop shaking the nail keg while constantly reminding me to stop asking so many questions. I was afraid Ken would cause the nail keg to roll toward the driver's side of the truck and cause our dad to return to our farm out of disgust. At one point, torrential rains forced Daddy to pull over to an old dilapidated filing station. It was in the middle of the night and, of course, we had no air conditioning in the truck back then. Mother had to sit there with Kenny on the nail keg between her knees and me by her side, while the rain pelted the windshield of our truck. With no air conditioning, the truck quickly fogged up inside, so the humidity intensified. Daddy wasn't too thrilled to be so confined but the rain was coming down in buckets. However, we made the overnight trip in spite of the thunderous weather, arriving at Mama and Papa Slaten's house in Tampa late the next afternoon.

We stopped at the edge of the yard. Mama, who was bow legged and had just gotten a new tight perm, walked out   toward our truck with both hands on her hips. Without even saying hello, she commented: "What took you so long?" Poor Mother was waiting for Ken to get off the nail keg, which still rested between her legs. As it happened, Ken suffered the most damage from this shoestring trip; the backs of his thighs were raw from the continuous shifting of the nail keg. When he and Mother got out of the car, he could hardly walk and neither could Mother, who like Mama, was also slightly bow legged! They were both totally exhausted from the long, daunting journey.

Looking down at Mother's legs, everyone began laughing. Her cotton stockings must have been snagged a million times by the rough wood on the nail keg. Her bow legs looked as if she had sprouted feathers! For several years I was sure the reason Mother's legs were bowed was because of that nail keg and the Florida trip. It's no wonder I later identified with the "Beverly Hill-billies" of TV fame!

~ ~ ~ ~ ~ ~ ~ ~ ~~ ~ ~ ~

When I was about nine years old, our parents bought a 110 acre farm in DeKalb County, a few miles north on Highway 75. There was an old dilapidated house on the property but our father said he got a good deal. To say the house had structural problems was an understate-ment. We lived in the old farm house until our new home was completed in 1940. Daddy built our new home using lumber which he acquired through some kind of trade. He was an expert in making good deals! Our male rela-tives and neighbors pitched in as they often did back in those days when a house was under construction. Our new two-story home with a full basement was completed in record time. Daddy installed the electrical system and running water as well in our house; one of the first residences in the area to benefit from these conveniences (more on this in a future chapter). Dormer windows were featured in the upstairs girls' bedroom which opened onto the top of the front porch. There were two living areas, three bedrooms, a separate dining room, large kitchen, and a screened in back porch with a full basement.

The front lawn was landscaped with the assistance of the DeKalb County Agent, Mr. John Pate, a friend of our dad. We children had the arduous task of helping sprig the front yard with grass which Mr. Pate had recommended. We had fun helping dismantle the old house once we moved into the new one. The entire experience was incredible and we have many fond memories of living across the highway from Freeman's Chapel.

The entire surrounding countryside was known as Sand Mountain. The mailman still delivered our mail to the same address: Rural Route #3, Crossville, Alabama. The day he delivered the new Sears catalogue was a major event in our household. As a very young girl, I thought new babies were ordered from the Sears catalogue! I'd look at all the pictures and choose the baby that I wanted for our family. A new Sears catalogue meant placing the old catalogue in the outhouse for further use!

After we moved to our new home, we were delighted to finally have running water which actually came from a faucet in the kitchen. We couldn't believe water was literally coming out of the pipe right into our kitchen sink!

New Home at Freeman's Chapel

As children growing up on that farm on Sand Moun-tain during WWII, we collected scrap iron to sell to the government for the war effort. Specifically, finding parts of farmers' old plows was considered worth pass-ing along as the iron could be used. We'd search in the fields and in the dirt around the house. We were paid a small amount but those pennies were like gold to us!

With the pennies we earned, we eagerly awaited the arrival of the country store peddler, Mr. Homer Woods, who made regular rounds in his "rolling store." We en-joyed climbing into the store, which was mounted low on the back of a truck bed. The inside shelves were stocked with basic cooking needs such as large bags of flour, fabrics and sewing notions along with our favorite candies. It was a treat to see the rolling store slowly moving down the road toward our house.

Mother bartered her fresh eggs, butter, and chick-ens with the peddler for items she needed from those shelves. We looked forward to buying a candy bar with our pennies from selling scrap iron or cotton we had picked. We spent much time in making the right selec-tion. I still remember a three color coconut bar (strawberry, vanilla, and chocolate) as being my favorite.

And, I recently learned that Cracker Barrel now sells those candy bars in their restaurants!

The rolling store is now obsolete but the memories linger as if it were yesterday. Mother purchased our flour in twenty-five pound white cloth bags. Later, those white flour bags were replaced by pretty floral patterns which after being washed were used for sewing dresses for the ladies of the house.

When I was nine, I remember wearing a dress Mother sewed using flour sack fabric with a floral design. While I liked the dress very much, I had such fear that the wind might blow my dress up to reveal matching panties!

My father grew cotton, corn and sorghum cane on our farm located on Highway 75 in northeast Alabama, between Albertville and Fort Payne. Since World War II was in progress, many items were rationed. Mother could purchase only minimal amounts of sugar which she used in canning, so sorghum syrup became a staple to replace the rationed sugar. I remember Mother pouring sorghum syrup over sweet potatoes as they cooked which resulted in delicious candied yams; also, she used the syrup in baking cookies. I vividly remember coming home from school on the bus, dashing through the front door and smelling those cookies fresh from the oven. Eating a few tea cakes, as we called them, and drinking a glass of cold milk while reading the comics in the newspaper were exciting events after school. I feverishly followed the characters in Little Orphan Annie, Dick Tracey, Dagwood and Blondie, Mary Worth, Gasoline Alley and Winnie Winkle back in those days.

Mother made laundry soap by boiling animal fats, water and lye in the same big black iron pot that she used for heating the water for doing the laundry. After cooking this soap mixture for a certain length of time, she poured the thickened concoction out onto a board to cool and "set." Later she cut the firm soap into squares for use in our weekly laundry. Because it contained lye, the soap was too strong for personal use, but great for the laundry.....a great shoestring project!

My dad worked hard on our farm to eke out a living for our family. I remember the day Pearl Harbor was bombed by the Japanese, December 7, 1941, which was the beginning of World War II. I was ten years old and with my dad at our nearby syrup mill. My Uncle Bethel came up to Daddy and said, "Vernal, the Japs have bombed Pearl Harbor!" And in his southern drawl, my dad replied, "Well, I'll be dad-blamed!" I was standing next to him and vividly remember the moment. I feared my dad might be drafted into the military service, but as a father of four he was exempted. During WWII, many young men in our community were called to serve in some branch of the military.

Our limited travels included an occasional week-end visit to folks who were relatives, friends, church connections, and/or business friends connected to our family's syrup making business. We children were excited just to ride along regardless. I don't ever recall being left at home alone.

I've always been intrigued by the interesting names of our Alabama relatives. Daddy's name was Vernal Tidmore Cobb. His parents were David and Nancy Tidmore Cobb and his siblings were Arlie, Myrtle, Bethel, Breman and Vola.

Mother's relatives lived on Sand Mountain and also in Florida. Mother's name was Pally Martisha Slaten (Tisha) and her siblings were Juanita, Bernice and Sibert. Mother's parents were Nettie and Albert Slaten, whom we called Mama & Papa Slaten. I fondly remember Uncle John and Aunt Becky Slaten (for whom our daughter, Becky, is named). I remember hearing a relative once say, "Aunt Becky keeps such a clean house, you could eat her biscuits right off the floor!"

There were many Rogers Sisters/Cousins! Here are a few more interesting names: James Rogers and Jo-anna Dyer had the following children: Nettie (my grandmother, Mama Slaten), Evie, Jessie, Bitha, Tugalo, Tombs and Florrie.

The children of Tugalo (above) were: Burma (the mother of Mel Tillis), Erma, Lila Dean, Woodrow, Mozelle, Virginia, Lois and their brother, J.T. We learned these names before telephones and other means of communication were available. Also, family reunions brought relatives closer in those days.

We enjoyed many family reunions and of course, the children listened to the adult conversations during this time. When there was a reunion, all the moms would be in the kitchen setting up tables with delicious home-cooked foods which they had prepared. The men would be outside in the yard, usually sitting under a big tree, discussing their crops, the status of the war, and the economic conditions of our country. There were no telephones, cell phones, no texting or computers. So, we children played tag, kick the can, and hide 'n seek. The girls also enjoyed skipping rope while the boys played marbles. I remember seeing a piano or organ in almost every relative's home. Music was a common bond which we all enjoyed. It's no wonder many of our relatives have inherited musical talents from that rich heritage. That was life on Sand Mountain back in the 1930's and 1940's!

Even today, music is still prevalent and has provided a common bond among generations. In fact, many members of our extended families have careers in music. First of all, we are proud to call Mel Tillis and his talented family our cousins! Our daughter, Susan, is an accomplished flutist and currently completing her doctorate in musical arts at the University of Oklahoma. Our son, David, plays guitar and sings. He and his other sister, Becky, often sing duets in church where he is in charge of music in College Station, Texas. David also enjoys blue grass, jazz and other genres on his guitar.

My brother, Ken, had his own little dance band in high school even though their musical catalogue was limited at that age. In addition to performing with his high school and college bands, Ken has also sung with his church choir. My sister, Mary, continues to sing with her church choir and our deceased sister, Jackie, and I were both choir members for years and I continue to enjoy my piano. Both my parents also played the piano. Yes, music makes the world go 'round!

The common bond of music between relatives will always be strong. This makes for great family gatherings! In fact, our David is bringing his favorite guitar and amplifier, mike, and music to our home for his dad's upcoming birthday weekend. He very generously accompanies me on his guitar as I sing songs from the forties and fifties into his fancy mike! I'm still a Patti Page "wantabee"! Our daughters, Susan and Becky, will contribute flute music and vocals as well.

As a proud Mom, I'd like to invite you to check out a song written and sung by our son, David Skinner, on www.youtube.com called "Alive in El Paso." He and wife Cindy were waiting at the airport in El Paso for their son, John, to return from a tour in Iraq. You'll see John's fiancé, Katie, and Cindy's parents as they greet John. John and Katie are now married and John was recently promoted to Captain in the Texas Army National Guard.

Happiness on a Shoestring

INTERESTING FACTS

On the day I was born.........
Top News Headlines on February 18th, 1931:

Feb 20 - Congress allows California to build the
Oakland- Bay Bridge

Feb 21 - Alka Seltzer was introduced

Feb 21 - Chicago White Sox & New York
Giants play the first exhibition
night game

Mar 3 - "Star Spangled Banner" officially
becomes U.S. national anthem

Top Songs for 1931:

Mood Indigo, Duke Ellington

Come to Me, BG DeSylva

I Apologize, Al Hoffman

Out of Nowhere, E. Heyman

Delicious, Ira Gershwin

All of Me, Seymour Simons

Heartaches, John Klenner

Ooh That Kiss, Mort Dixon

1931 Prices:

Bread:	$0.08/loaf
Milk:	0.50/gal
Eggs:	0.50/doz
Car:	$530.00
House:	$6,796
Ave. Income:	$1,527
DOW Avg:	78

U.S. President: Herbert Hoover

U.S. Vice-President: Charles Curtis

Academy Award Winners for 1931:

Best Picture:	Cimarron
Best Actor:	Lionel Barrymore in "Free Soul"
Best Actress:	Marie Dressler in "Min and Bill"

Famous people born on February 18th:

1920 Jack Palance

1933 Yoko Ono Lennon

1950 Sybil Shepherd

1954 John Travolta

Happiness on a Shoestring

2

Memories at Painter

Mrs. Light's Class

When we moved into our new home in DeKalb County, Alabama, we were in a different school district. Children in grades one through eight were required to attend nearby Painter School. My older two sisters, Mary and Jackie, continued their studies at Crossville High School. My most memorable time at Painter was in the sixth, seventh and eighth grades in the 1940's. All three grades were combined in one room and our teacher was Mrs. Ora Light. There were about twenty students in this room. Mrs. Light was an excellent teacher and responsible for creating a library in one corner of our classroom using shoestring ideas. We painted an old table white as well as some empty nail kegs which we used for seats around the table. We also painted several orange crates white to hold our new library books which Mrs. Light had acquired. That small library motivated me to enjoy reading. During those years, I remember reading *Little Women*, the *Five Little Peppers* series, the *Nurse Jane Barton* series, as well as many other books. I also remember the boys enjoying the Zane Grey books.

Every morning at the beginning of class, we had a short Bible reading and repeated the Pledge of Allegiance. Oft times, I would sing a little solo such as "Mairzy Dotes," "Sentimental Journey," or "America."

In the center of the room, there was a large pot belly stove filled with coal during the winter months to heat the class room. The boys in our class took turns bringing in a scuttle of coal from the outside. Whenever I watch the TV program, "Little House on the Prairie," I think, "That's Painter!"

Classmates I remember during those years include: Catherine Isom, Evelyn Bearden, Sarah Jane Painter, Winfred Stevens, Charles Gilliland, Buell Wilkes, Charles Gardner, Edward King, James Russell, Imogene O'Shields, Lucille Cooper, Juanee Martin, Mary Alice and Earline Wilkes, RC and Kermit Hammonds, Imogene Cooper, Harold and Corine Holsonback, Edna Grace Williams, Inez West, and Helen Davis. Other names escape me, but I remember most of the faces in the picture.

Our first assignment in Mrs. Light's class on "Occupational Guidance" was to decide on a vocation. As I lay in bed that night, I couldn't decide whether

I wanted to be a nurse or a teacher. I was excited to be thinking of my potential and this particular class helped me make initial decisions which I actually accomplished. When graduating from college, I held in my hand a teaching degree and I remembered the exact moment that decision to teach was made. I later taught school at an army military base in Germany when my husband was stationed there.

The five room school at Painter where my brother, Ken, and I attended was on the road leading to Fort Payne. As each student completed the eighth grade, they could transfer to Crossville High School if they desired or complete ninth grade at Painter. I chose to transfer to Crossville for ninth grade and enjoyed being in a real high school!

REFLECTIONS: I cherish my memories of the days spent at Painter. My special friend, Buell, and I exchanged many notes during this time but we rarely talked in person. There was no television, no phones, no emails, no computers, no texting, no hair spray, no spray starch or any other conveniences. But, God was honored every day in our schools and churches, we loved our country and each other, and I feel honored to have this background and appreciate all the people on Sand Mountain who were a part of my life through those years.

3

Demise of the Outhouse

A memorable occasion at the Painter School happened the day the girl's outside toilet caved in! As we reached the school playground that fateful morning, the earlier arrivals were already talking about the demise of the familiar little building. Of course, we were all in a rush to see this unheard of disaster.

As we neared the area at the back of the school, on the west side of the gymnasium, we were absolutely stunned to see the rooftop slanted backwards. All six stalls with surrounding wooden fence were leaning backwards, too, slanting into the earth with only the edges of the seats visible! The giggling boys thought this was the most amazing thing to ever happen at Painter. And, the girls were warned to not even think of going near the mired mess. Then, we began to wonder if perhaps we might get to miss a few days of school until a new facility was built. The only sure thing we knew, we were NOT to go near the area at all! School was not cancelled, sad to say.

In future days, the girls and boys alternated using the boy's toilet located on the opposite side of the gymnasium. Now, this was a new experience for us, because we girls had never seen a boy's urinal. Back in the 1940's, this was our initial introduction to the birds and the bees. In due time, a new outhouse for the girls was built ~ life was simple, very simple, in those days.

More Memories at Painter

The Painter School is no longer in existence; however, the area holds many fond memories for those of us who studied there. We enjoyed basketball most of all and cheered on our team. I remember playing softball with the other students on the playground and, if we wanted to bat, we had to work our way up from third base. We advanced to the next position as the outs were made.

To reach our school every day, we rode the Crossville school bus to the Howard Store at Painter. We then walked on to the school which was a short distance. The bus then took the older students on to Crossville, several miles down a long, country road. As we waited for the afternoon bus to pick us up at the store, we often bought a candy bar if we had a nickel in our pocket. I loved the Pay Day and Powerhouse candy bars best. As we waited for that afternoon bus to take us home, I remember playing jack stones on the concrete porch at Howard's store. Inez West was a whiz with those jacks!

I fondly remember one morning as I was walking across the school grounds to the building my friend, Lucille Cooper, ran out to meet me. As she was running across the playground, her maroon and white striped broomstick skirt came undone at the waist and it floated down to the ground like a balloon ~ those were the days!

The Painter Community Center has now replaced the site where the school once stood. This is where the "V" Flag of World War II, mentioned in upcoming pages of this book, is now displayed.

My parents first met at Painter School many, many years ago, so the area holds a special place in my heart. They both taught school there. After their marriage, they lived at Crossville where Mother taught school and Daddy worked at the Gaines Department Store.

Happiness on a Shoestring

4

Freeman's Chapel Memories

Freeman's Chapel, the little church across the high-way from our house, was a meeting place on Sunday for the neighbors in our community. We attended church every Sunday morning and "singing" every Sunday night. The second Sunday of each month was the day the preacher came and delivered a scathing sermon in our little church out in the country. My dad conducted the singings and taught all of us many new songs from the latest song book each summer during our two week "singing school." The two weeks ended with a concert on the last Friday night, which was well attended by the people in the community. Many churches dotted the communities on Sand Mountain and the social lives of our families generally centered on church activities.

Our preacher, Brother Conway, was a respected man of God in our community. He wore little elastic arm bands to keep his long shirt sleeves pushed up. Since there was no air conditioning at that time, he really per-spired as he pounded the top of the pulpit to make a point! However, as a young girl, I thought he preached way too long! He usually ate lunch with our family afterwards.

During World War II, the entire community was behind the war effort and we supported our troops in every possible way. Some ladies in our church made a flag of white material, the edges bound in red and a large "V" in the center featuring one side of the "V" in blue and the other in red. Each family or friend considered it an honor to stitch their serviceman's name on a blue cloth star and place it on the outer edge of the "V". This flag was hung up front inside the church.

Flag Honoring our Military in WWII

There were forty-nine names of local men on the flag. Three did not return ~ Vernon Mayes and Boyce Pointer were killed in action. L. W. Painter was reported missing in action and was never found. Their stars were removed and placed inside the "V". The flag was found in the attic of Freeman Church approximately forty years later and framed by the Painter Home Demonstration ladies and it continues to hang in the Painter Community Center today. The above exemplified the patriotism exhibited in our Community during that time. I appreciate the assistance of my dear friend, Colene Wilkes Morgan, concerning the information about this memorable flag.

On a sadder note, one of the men killed in action, Vernon Mayes, lived with our family for several years when he was a young boy, so this became a personal loss for us. At the end of each Sunday night singing, we usually ended our service by singing, "Waiting For The Boys To Come Home." Times were tough then, but there was a sweet spirit in the place. Our small one room church was an important focal point in the community and even today, it still remains so.

The church has received many improvements over the years including additional space.

We came to appreciate gospel music during this time. I have fond memories of the all day singings at Freeman and "dinner on the ground" outside under the trees. The food was actually served on lined up church benches covered with table cloths.

In addition to the Christmas programs, our main program of the year was always the second Sunday in May which we referred to as "Decoration Day," which included a covered dish dinner along with the sermon and lots of singing. People brought beautiful flower arrangements to decorate their loved one's graves. Each family brought their favorite foods to be shared at lunch.

During the church service all mothers were honored. If one's mother was deceased, a white flower was worn and if the mother were still alive a red flower was worn.

We enjoyed the singing, especially since we knew all the songs. And then, the noontime meal was the highlight of the day and enjoyed by all. I was especially passionate about the delicious cakes made from Swans Down Cake Flour because they were finely textured (this was before cake mixes). Mother's cakes were relatively bland compared to those baked with Swans Down Cake Flour. I remember asking my mother why she didn't use Swans Down Cake Flour and her staunch quick reply was, "We can't afford it!" We didn't question our parents in those days. I vividly remember the extreme headaches I experienced after those "dinner on the ground" Sundays. The only food I ever ate on that day was the Swans Down Cake and as much as possible! I always suffered piercing headaches after these fabulous events ~ looking back, I simply had a sugar high. But, I must say, it was worth it!

Famous gospel singers from nearby Nashville often made guest appearances at those all day singings. My two older sisters, little brother and I were regularly called upon the stage to sing in a quartet fashioned by our dad. Ken was about six years old and I was about eight. The audience loved it when we sang, "I'll Fly Away" because Ken added "......in the morning" at the end in a deep voice which everyone enjoyed.

My Nashville cousin, Daisy Bell Littlejohn, often came down for these big events at our church. She was trim, attractive, and very friendly. When she sat down on the piano bench to play, everyone took notice ~ she could play the piano like no other! I remember sitting down at our own piano the following week trying to play like Daisy Bell! However, my best number at that time was "Chop Sticks"! I later perfected one of Daisy Bell's specials, "All the Day Long," which was a catchy tune! If you like gospel music, you may remember this one.

A few years later, the neighborhood teenage boys came to the Sunday night singings at Freeman and sat in the audience while we young girls were on the stage singing. However, we kept our eyes open watching to see where they sat, which was usually near the back, and perhaps share a smile or two.

During my preteen years, I walked across the highway to the church every mid-week, swept the floor and made sure all the song books were properly stored. I made it my weekly responsibility to keep the church in order for the Sunday services though no one else knew this. When I became lonely, I would go over to the church and spend some time "with Jesus" as I came to rely on Him. I felt He loved me even though I was a girl when my parents were hoping for a boy, He loved me even though I was too tall for my age, and He loved me even though I talked too much ~ He loved me just the way I was!

After the entire church was in order, I then stepped up to the pulpit and delivered a scathing sermon to the empty audience! I would remind everyone what would happen if they were bad ~ they would surely have to walk on red hot chains in hell and I amplified on that in as many ways as I could possibly imagine! How I wish I had tapes of my "sermons" ~ Brother Conway would have been proud of me!

The birth order played a significant role in my life. My two older sisters, Mary and Jackie, were twenty months apart in age and about five and six years older than I. They always had their own teenage agenda.

I knew my parents were hoping for a son when I was born because others often reminded me. In addition, I grew tall at an early age and well-meaning neighbors would comment, "Bonnie Jean, you're so tall you should have been a boy because that's what your folks wanted!" And I was often told, "Don't talk so much and ask so many questions!" I was often lonely because there were few girls my age in our neighborhood and my mother was always busy with many chores. And, my sisters were always doing things together so I really felt lonely most of the time. Also, I was weary of being called "Bonnie Jean" because I liked being called by my first name only, but no one would do that.

From these experiences, I always tried to be available to our three children as they grew up. If you're too busy for your own children when they need you, you may need to rethink your priorities. And I hope our children will remember the fun we have had! Courtesies extended are a good investment. It takes so little to make someone else feel special. I would like to recommend an excellent book by my dear friend, Florence Littauer, *"It Takes So Little To Be Above Average!"* It'll change your life.

At Freeman's Chapel the Sunday School classes were divided by the church benches in the one big, single meeting room. I vividly remember where I sat each year depending on my age. In the earlier grades, I could hardly wait to get my Sunday School card each Sunday from the teacher. I knew there would be a colored picture on one side of the card, usually of Jesus interacting with children or other worshippers. On the other side of the card there would be a line of scripture, a short story, and then at the bottom there would be a memory verse. I cherished those cards and kept all of them in the top drawer of my chest of drawers upstairs. When I became sad or discouraged in my family, I knew I could always go upstairs, get out my cards and talk to Jesus. I vividly remembered all the memory verses and stories on every card and that made a lasting impression on that little girl.

THE SERMON ON THE MOUNT.
Why call ye me, Lord, Lord, and do not the things which I say?

NO. 1. FEBRUARY 9, 1895.   DAVID C. COOK PUBLISHING CO., CHICAGO.

One day, after looking at all my cards, I decided to make Jesus my very best friend forever and ever. I knew He loved me even though I was tall for my age, He loved me even though I was a girl when my family wanted a boy when I was born, and He loved me even though I talked too much ~ HE LOVED ME JUST THE WAY I WAS! When I put all my cards back in the top drawer, I walked back down the stairs, feeling like a million dollars! I remember that from that day forward, Jesus would always be my BEST friend and He loved me just as I was. During summer revivals I wondered why people became so emotional as they pondered their relationship with the Lord. I distinctly remember the day I stood at my chest of drawers and made a strong decision to always keep Jesus first in my life and that's exactly the way it's always been. I am reminded of this every time I see a Sunday School Card of any kind!

DECORATION DAY AT FREEMAN'S CHAPEL

I was always captivated by beautiful city flowers and as a child I eagerly looked forward to Decoration Day at our little church across the highway. It was a family tradition to visit the cemetery and place flowers on the graves of loved ones now gone. I knew the "country" flowers, those grown on the farms, would quickly wilt; however, the "city" flowers, from the florist, were very special and lasted much longer. I was fascinated by anything from the city!

One Decoration Day when I was a young girl about nine years old, I returned to the cemetery after everyone had gone. As I walked around the graves identifying the city flowers, I noticed a small baby's grave with no flowers at all. So, I "borrowed" some pink carnations from a nearby grave and other pink flowers from various graves to completely cover the small, bare mound. As I stood admiring my handiwork, I noticed other barren graves, so I decorated them as well. I decorated some graves in solid colors, some with a mixed variety of flowers, and others with fancy greenery.

Bonnie,
Nine Years Old

Finally, I was satisfied with my work and as I scanned the cemetery, I was expecting to see a beautiful array of flowers neatly divided among the graves. Instead, I was horrified to see gaping holes of missing flowers in the larger arrangements. It was obvious that in my eagerness to share the flowers, I'd made an absolute mess. I had to borrow and balance as much as possible so my rearrangements would not be so evident. It must have taken two hours or more.

Satisfied that I had tidied up the cemetery sufficiently, I selected about ten long stemmed white gladiolus for my very own. Clutching the massive "glads," I walked around the graves as I sang, "I come to the garden alone, while the dew is still on the roses....and He walks with me and He talks with me, and He tells me I am His own!" As I sang to all the graves, I felt quite spiritual and realized that I really belonged to Jesus. I felt He was pleased to hear me singing to each grave and that I had given an equal amount of flowers to everyone. He was even pleased that I saved some "glads" for myself!

Feeling somewhat spiritual, I knew Jesus wouldn't mind if I took "my own gladiolus" home with me, so I did. I walked across the highway to our home carrying the flowers as if I were a bride. At home, I placed them in Mother's best vase on the dining table and went out to play with my little brother, satisfied that I had contributed to our home décor.

It wasn't long before I heard Mother's strong, demanding voice say: "WHO brought these flowers into this house?" Seeing my face, it was clear she need look no further. As I clutched my cherished "glads" with frightened hands, Mother literally dragged me across the highway to the church cemetery and yelled, "Now, you put those flowers back where you found them!"

With a wild look of disbelief, Mother surveyed my damage to the cemetery. "What have you done, Bonnie Jean?" she screamed. She could not believe one of her "precious children" had made such a mess of the entire cemetery. Even at that point, I realized there were still large empty spaces in some of the "city flower" arrangements. Her next words were, "Bonnie Jean, get me a switch right NOW!" When she used both my names, I knew I was in serious trouble. Have you ever had to get a "switch"? It's difficult to find an appropriate one in a cemetery. She yanked the leaves off backwards on the least offending switch I could find, tossing the leaves hither and yon behind her and then she ordered, "Now, you get over here!"

That event ended my redecorating days, but the memory of that expanse of flowers and my personal arrangement of "glads" is a picture I will keep in my mind forever, along with a smile on my face and a song in my heart. Even today, "In The Garden" is still my favorite hymn!

Another fond memory of the many times I visited that cemetery was when I simply walked around reading the names and dates on the tomb stones. We knew many of the families represented. Sometimes I would pull a weed from a grave or straighten the flowers a loved one might have brought earlier.

There was one grave marker made of white marble that I distinctly remember above all the others. The largest part of the white marble base was about fourteen by sixteen inches and about four inches tall. The next square of marble on top of the base was a few inches smaller but slightly taller. The next section was still smaller but much taller, approximately fifteen inches tall. On the top of the entire tomb stone there was a small slanted base of carved marble resembling an open Bible and I could barely see the "open page". As a little girl I remember standing barefoot on one of those ledges and holding on tightly while I pretended to read out of that marble Bible to all the graves. I felt closer to God there than any place else on Sand Mountain.

Bonnie at Tombstone Today

Throughout my adult life, I have made it a family tradition to take my children, and now my grandchildren, to that cemetery when we are back in Alabama. Several years ago my childhood friend in Alabama, Colene, sent me an email saying she had been walking by that cemetery recently and stopped to make sure her parents and brother's graves were in good condition. She thought of me and just wanted to let me know and today, she is still one of my dearest Sand Mountain friends!

Sad to say, our home across the highway from Freeman's Chapel was recently replaced by a new highway but at least the church still stands. However, it is impossible to erase the memories there from my childhood ~ especially the rooftop memories, Freeman's Chapel, the Swans Down Cakes and Decoration Day ~ all which I will forever cherish!

5

Life on Sand Mountain

My parents were hard working people and in the 1940's life became more serious as our country became engaged in WWII. I could tell by my dad's demeanor of his deep concern as he diligently read the newspapers and listened for daily radio reports on our sole radio in the living room. He scrimped and saved in his work at the syrup mill and in all his responsibilities. I have fond memories of watching him use a hammer to straighten a bent nail for reuse.

My mother tended to the household responsibilities and always planted a huge vegetable garden at the edge of our yard. We children didn't have specific chores; we simply did what was needed to be done at any given time. Bringing in wood for mother's kitchen stove was a constant chore and we usually had to check our arms for splinters after each load. In addition to providing heat for cooking, the right end of our kitchen stove featured a built-in reservoir which held several gallons of water, also heated by the fire. This served as warm dish washing water.

It was a memorable day when our new house featured hot and cold running water. Bringing in buckets of water from the outside well for kitchen use was not on my list of favorite things to do. In earlier days, we took our baths in a #2 wash tub, which necessitated more trips with buckets of water. Mother hung the laundry outside on long clothes lines.

We children had to pick cotton, work in the cane fields, take water to the men plowing the fields, and help wash all of mother's empty glass Ball fruit jars for canning. Every summer Mother took pride in preserving her home grown vegetables in hundreds of jars for her growing family. These jars were lined up as if we had our own grocery store down in our basement.

I hasten to add one additional memory ~ Mother always canned many jars of beets and I wondered why, since no one in our family seemed to like them; also, they looked pale and anemic! I later learned the way to make them have a richer color was to add food coloring and then they became a deep, rich red becoming more palatable. When I asked her why she didn't use food coloring, she quickly replied, "We can't afford food coloring" so that was that. She always had a definitive answer for everything. One season Mother canned a record 1200 jars of food. As I said, she did everything with gusto!

Our big back yard always had a flock of clucking chickens wandering aimlessly around looking for morsels of food. When Mother needed a chicken for dinner, she simply tossed a handful of corn out in the yard to those unsuspecting birds as they scurried around enjoying the feast. With her hands resting on her hips, she made her choice. I'll spare the "gusto" she exuded here. That's the way mother selected her chicken for our Sunday meal as well, especially if the Preacher would be eating with us. Both Mother and Mama Slaten had "gusto"!

In the late nineteen thirties, Mama came up from Tampa to visit one summer. With four children in tow, Mother stayed extremely busy, so Mama decided to pitch in and help get the entire house in order before she returned to Tampa. She collected all the debris, or what she considered debris, and piled it into a heap in the back yard and lit a match! To my utter dismay, I saw my little pot holder purse which I had lovingly made on a loom, go up in flames along with many other things "we didn't need" according to Mama. That little purse contained all my notes from Buell, and I decided that Mama was not to be trusted in the future!

WATERLOGGED!

One day my brother, Ken, and I were wandering around our farm looking for new adventures. We were about six and eight years old. There had been a tremendous rainstorm the night before and large puddles of water were everywhere. As we wandered into a nearby cotton field, we noticed our dad had added more dirt to a terrace row because the rains had flooded his growing cotton crop. To rebuild the terrace row, he had shoveled deep red dirt from a nearby area. This left a long, wide and rather deep section where more water had accumulated during the previous night. We decided to take our little "boats" sailing since there was plenty of puddles available!

After discarding the matches, we took the little match boxes (our "boats") down to the mud puddles to see if they would float. To our dismay, once the cardboard became soaked, our little "boats" sank! However, the water was so inviting, I said to my little brother, "If you'll push me down in this water, I'll do the same for you!" And that's exactly how our afternoon of fun began!

We discovered we could run and dive into the water and completely submerge ourselves. We had such fun because never before had we played in muddy water like that! Suddenly, Mother appeared with her usual "hands on her hips" stance. I attempted to stand up straight but still remember my maroon slacks were literally drooping on me because the pockets were full of muddy muck! I was wearing a white blouse but when I looked down at that blouse, it was muddy ugly and I think that was my last time I ever wore it.

Ken's overall pockets were likewise full of muddy water, especially the little bib part up front which was completely full of mud. Mother tried to spank us both, but we could barely feel her hand. She then broke a switch from the nearby apple tree to "tan our hides" but that switch broke. She was trying not to laugh but failed miserably! Our hair and pockets were both full of that red mud but we had an amazing time!

I remember Mother removing Ken's little overalls and making him run to the house naked. Since I was "older" I didn't have to disrobe until we reached the backyard steps where Mother hosed me down!

This was our first experience of actually "diving" into water and for sure it's one of our fondest memories!

6

Mother's Sewing Machine

In those memorable days, Mother belonged to a newly organized Home Demonstration Club, which was part of the Farm Bureau. Along with other ladies in the community, she learned to make mattresses (most people in those days slept on feather beds or mattresses made of corn husks crammed into ticking). We were excited when her finished products arrived at our house. I still remember the fresh odor of the ticking and the fluffy cotton inside.

In addition to making mattresses, Mother learned how to repair our Singer sewing machine (the type with a floor pedal). Instructors from nearby Fort Payne came to the Painter Home Demonstration Club and helped the ladies with various projects. I was with Mother the day she attended this class. She took the demo Singer apart, oiled the parts as directed, and then reassembled it to its original condition. (Mother said she took me with her so I could remember how it was done!) We were greatly impressed with the results.

The next day at home, we carefully disassembled Mother's precious Singer as we had been instructed the previous day. We cleaned and oiled all the parts and with great care laid out all the pieces on the table in the order removed. Next, we put all the pieces back into the machine as prescribed. Things went well and we were pleased by our abilities to follow the teacher's instructions; however, at the end of our project, we discovered we had <u>one piece remaining</u> ~ our beloved Singer machine was never the same!

Back in the days before Mother "overhauled" her Singer sewing machine, she sewed with gusto. She peddled that machine so fast I expected her to stitch right across one of her fingers at any time. She did everything with gusto and sewing was no exception. I remember Mother was sewing one day and she told me to watch my little brother, who was about three at the time, while she sewed her dress. Even at age five, I thought she should sew slower; however, she zoomed along with the foot pedal going up and down very fast on her Singer sewing machine as she directed the fabric underneath the needle. She was sewing the pretty floral fabric that originally served as a bag for flour from

the peddler mentioned earlier, a shoestring way to add to one's wardrobe.

Mother finished a long side seam and pulled the half-finished dress over her head for a fitting. She quickly yanked the garment down over her shoulders but it would go no further than around her breasts. She gasped and yelled for one of my older sisters to come, "Get the scissors, quick!" she panted. In one fell swoop, she quickly cut the bunched garment away from her chest and tossed the unfinished dress into the waste basket as she deeply inhaled her seemingly final breath. As I said, Mother did everything with gusto!

I learned numerous and valuable lessons from my parents ~ the importance of economizing, how to make do with what we had on hand, how to dream, plan, think ahead and work hard in order to achieve our dreams and goals.

⋯⋯ and, the importance of taking sewing lessons!

7

Sand Mountain Memories

My little brother, Ken, and I had few toys so we often improvised. We rolled old tires or inner tubes around our back yard as we pretended to go "to town." We would announce that we were going to Painter, Crossville, Geraldine, Fort Payne, Fyffe, Albertville, Boaz, Gadsden or perhaps Birmingham (if we had enough gas!) and we would "travel" around our big yard and talk about what we "saw" en route!

Our hands and clothes would get very dirty to our mother's chagrin. More importantly, at about 6 and 8 years of age, we often talked about how we hated all the farm work to be done. My most vivid memories center around the times Ken and I made plans to leave the farm and head to the city as soon as possible since we disliked the farm life, more specifically the farm chores.

One hot, summer day we were tasked with taking a load of corn up to Mr. Bearden's grist meal so he could grind it into meal for Mother to make corn bread. We were about eight and ten years old at that time and were not too motivated to walk up the hot, sandy road barefoot, coaxing the mule to pull the "slide" carrying those bags of corn. The distance was about a half mile but walking barefoot in the hot sand was almost impossible. These were the days before there were all kinds of tennis shoes available, so we children went barefoot during the summer months except for attending church or going to other places. We always looked forward to getting new shoes for school in September!

On our way back home with the freshly ground corn meal in the bags, I shared with my brother that I was thinking of running away from home. After hearing my story, he replied, "Me, too!" We agreed, we were tired of all this heavy work. That night as we gathered at the supper table, Ken told the family what I had said. Everyone laughed and I felt ridiculous. I then told my family, "Well, when I said I was leaving home, Kenny said, "Me, too!'" And, we jokingly called him "me, too" after that!

~ ~ ~ ~ ~ ~ ~ ~ ~ ~ ~ ~

During cotton picking season, Ken and I always picked just enough cotton to make our sacks comfortable enough to lie on and daydream. As we watched the white fluffy clouds slowly move overhead, I would search for the perfect cloud resembling a white poodle and I would talk about having a white poodle when I moved to the city. (Many years later, this dream came true, I had a little white poodle named Nikki and I often told her how very lucky she was!)

During the syrup season, playing on the sorghum cane pummy pile was one of our favorite things to do. Pummies are cane stalks that have been pressed through a grinder to extract all the juices needed for

Bonnie and Ken at a cane pile. Our house in the back.

making syrup; the stalks become limp and quickly pile up once they have gone through the grinder. Even though this was our favorite pastime, the bees bothered us constantly. They loved the sweet smell of the cane juice and we were often stung but we still enjoyed performing aerial acrobatics knowing we would be landing in the soft pummies below! As the farmers brought their cane to our mill for processing the pummy pile grew larger and larger providing a great playground for turning flips. Turning flips on the pummies and someday swimming like Esther Williams were my two obsessions as a young girl!

Other things occupying our young lives: Tag, Marbles, Hide & Seek, Rover Red Rover, Baseball, and Kick the Can. The girls enjoyed using old pine needles for our make-believe "furniture" in floor plans, outlined with sticks, on the pasture's green grass.

One sunny afternoon my dear friend and neighbor, Mary Alice Wilkes, and I decided to make some "snuff" which we had seen being used by older women in our area. We substituted cocoa and sugar for the horribly tasting snuff and we made some little brushes from twigs underneath our "secret tree" for dipping. We stuffed the make believe snuff inside our lower lips and spit through our two fingers just as the older women did ~ we had such fun!

The boys went skinny dipping in the creek but the girls weren't allowed! Do you have any memorable childhood stories you could share with others? It's a good thing!

My brother, Ken, and I daydreamed all the time in our early years. He is now a retired Air Force Colonel and was recently featured in the Sand Mountain Reporter in Alabama, as being honored for his military service during the Viet Nam War. His F4 Phantom Jet was shot down in Viet Nam but he successfully bailed out and was rescued. He continues to fly and enjoys his own private hanger and planes in Guntersville, Alabama. Needless to say, I'm very proud of him!

Below are four generations of the Cobb Family, 1954. Steve (the infant) is now a retired AF pilot like his Dad, Ken, who is holding him. Our Dad is in the center and Grandad William David Cobb, is at right.

During our preteen years, our horizons were greatly expanded, for whatever reason we did not realize at the time. Little did we know that Daddy's professional working relationship with Mr. John Lowery, an Agronomist at Auburn University, would provide a means to develop new varieties and hybrids of sorghum syrup. And, now many years later, my brother and Mr. Lowery's son have become friends through their common interests in aviation.

The Outhouse Caper

Our imaginations were quite vivid and on one occasion Ken and I exercised our freedom a bit too much. Back in the early nineteen forties, it was common to see a small building isolated behind each house in our farming community. This strategically placed little building was known as the "outhouse." Few country homes built during this time frame had indoor plumbing. Consequently, we made a mad dash to the outhouse when nature called. Most of the outhouses were built with two holes which were affectionately known as a "two-seater."

Ken and I were wandering around our farm looking for our next adventure. When our parents bought the farm, there was an old shabby house where we lived until our new house was completed. The even shabbier outhouse was still standing nearby and it was here that Ken and I had a memorable experience.

The old outhouse door was ajar and vacant. As we walked by Ken looked inside and made a snide remark about the excrement below as he glanced into one of the open holes. I looked in and verbally agreed with him and added a new adjective. He then continued to add other words and so did I. We didn't know many naughty words as we were quite young but we used the ones we had heard our father use when he was plowing and would get mad at the mules! Nevertheless, that didn't keep us from continuing our conversation. Neither of us had ever said a naughty word to each other because we knew Mother would spank us. As a former school teacher before marrying our dad, she had trained us well. However, on that day Ken and I were in new territory and we were having such fun!

We were so amazed at our outburst of naughty words, we never told ANYONE! On the other hand, when we got into scrapes or arguing about something, we could control the other person by simply threatening to tell Mother "what you said!" So, that would end the quarrel every time.

Time passed and our own children were grown, so we felt it would be a good time to tell Mother this story. It was several years before her death when we finally confessed our "sin" to her. As in former days, she raised her head and sternly looked up at us and said, "You both should be ashamed of yourselves!" We were, but it was fun. To this day (and we're both in our seventies now), we only have to mention the word, "outhouse," and we become hysterical!

8

Rooftop Antics

As preteens, my brother and I were always bored as we wandered around the farm looking for things to do. We secretly climbed on top of our two-story home many times by going through the upstairs dormer windows leading to the top of the front porch and then crawling on to the top of the roof. We could see forever!

And so, as you may imagine by now, I also spent quite a bit of time on our rooftop alone because that was the one safe place I could be without interruption.

As a twelve year old, one of my favorite things to do after the regular Sunday night singings at Freeman's Chapel was to rush back home across the highway in the dark, hurry up the stairs, climb out the window and stand on top of the porch. From that vantage point, I could see who was walking home with whom! Living across the highway from the church had numerous advantages.

Other times, I secretly climbed out the dormer window and then carefully crawled on up to the rooftop, sitting regally and waving to passersby. On occasion, I pretended to be the Queen and waved to the "little people" as Queen Elizabeth did in the newsreels at the Carol Theatre in nearby Albertville.

My most favorite thing to do was to pretend I was Dale Evans, the wife of Roy Rogers, who was my favorite person in the world next to my own dad. I would sing, "I'm Back in the Saddle Again," "Don't Fence Me In," and "Tumbling Tumbleweeds" as I perched on the rooftop waiting for Roy to come home for supper! Even today here in Norman, Oklahoma, I smile to think that we live only 350 miles from Branson, Missouri, where the Roy Rogers Museum is now located. Trigger the horse, Bullet the dog, Nelliebell the jeep, and all the other Roy Rogers artifacts are safely ensconced in that building. On one of our visits to Branson, Jack and I met Rusty Rogers, Roy's son who now headlines a show there. I was pleased to share with him my memory of when he was born and how I saved the newspaper clipping from the Birmingham News for years afterwards. That's fond memories on a shoestring.

On Sand Mountain we lived on a "sunup to sundown" schedule with no clock in sight. It was a quiet world after sunset. There was no television in those days, no bedtime stories, and we had only one radio. We woke up to the sound of roosters and went to sleep at night listening to cicadas through open windows. Without air conditioning, these sounds made going to sleep a bit more palatable on those hot Alabama nights. My husband, Jack, recently asked me what we children did after sunset. Without hesitating I said, "We caught lightning bugs and put them in jars or we chased bats with sticks!" I remember listening to "A Date With Judy" on the radio on Tuesday nights. Another fun thing we did during the day was catch June bugs and tie a string to one of the back legs and let them fly in circles. We always had "backup June bugs" because we often needed replacements!

A favorite event during the hot summer months in north Alabama was ice cream socials. My parents enjoyed making ice cream by the gallons. I believe our ice cream maker held two gallons and we often invited neighbors over to enjoy the festivities. Mother had collected many little "depression bowls" from detergent and cereal boxes through the years and those served as our dishes for the ice cream. Once Daddy filled the empty spaces around the ice cream container with crushed ice, he placed a folded burlap bag on top of the ice cream maker to keep the chill inside. Then, he began stirring the mixture with the hand crank. The burlap bag also served as a seat for a younger child for the purpose of helping to keep the ice cream maker stable while our dad cranked the handle. I can almost hear my dad say, "Be still, Bonnie Jean!" We knew the ice cream was about frozen when our dad had difficulty turning the handle and also when our bottoms seemed frozen as well!

At about age fourteen or fifteen, I was allowed to go to Albertville alone. This is one of my fondest memories. A commercial bus passed our house daily for the twelve mile ride, so this was a big treat for me.

For about two dollars I made more memories than one can imagine: I paid the bus driver a small amount for my ride, visited both dime stores on opposite sides of Main Street in Albertville and even at that age, I made sure everything was in order! I saved fifteen cents for a movie magazine, five cents for some hot chocolate and ten cents for a hamburger. I enjoyed sitting in the drug store on one of the revolving stools at the counter, reading my new magazine while eating my hamburger and drinking hot chocolate. I remember crossing my legs, tossing my long hair aside and thinking, "I am in downtown Albertville all by myself!" I enjoyed reading my new movie magazines ~ Photoplay and Motion Pictures were my favorites ~ and did I ever feel upscale!

I enjoyed reading about Betty Grable, Rita Hayworth, Liz Taylor, Jane Powell, Debbie Reynolds, Robert Wagner, Esther Williams, Doris Day, Tony Curtis and Natalie Wood. Since the drug store also served as the bus station, I was always fascinated as I watched the lady stamping bus tickets at the nearby booth and thought I might be able to get her job someday. Those trips to Albertville were memorable for me. I later pasted my walls with pictures from those movie magazines, especially the ones of Tony Curtis!

My favorite movie during this time was "State Fair," which was filmed in the late '40's. It was a story about a family who took their pet pig to the State Fair for judging and how he won the blue ribbon. The brother and sister in the film were about my age and they longed to go to the city and find new friends. Jeannie Crain played the sister and Dick Haymes the brother. She sat in her upstairs dormer window, wearing a white pinafore and singing "I keep wishing I were somewhere else, walking down a strange new street; hearing words that I have never heard, from a man I've yet to meet!" Oh, how I lived my life vicariously through that girl sitting in the window and many times I repeated that scene in my own upstairs bedroom later wearing my own white pinafore and singing that song. I longed to go to new places and do new things!

~~~~~~~~~~~~~~~~~~~~~~~

In time, I went to Montgomery with a fellow student, Kermit Hammonds. We were the two healthiest 4-H Club members in DeKalb County and were fortunate to ride on our county's float at the 1946 Inaugural Parade of the new Governor, "Big Jim" Folsom. We were in junior high and the only two people on the float as we rode through downtown Montgomery. Mother "made" me wear my first bra on that special day. At first I was mad but during the parade I stood straight and tall, thinking, "I'm probably the only girl in Montgomery wearing a new bra!" Poor Kermit never knew the rest of that story. This trip was a great experience for both of us at that time.

Bonnie and Kermit Hammonds

Because my dad was becoming a well-known sorghum syrup maker, it was important that our own sorghum cane be of exemplary quality. We children had to help chop the weeds away so the little plants could flourish. It seemed we were always working in the cane fields every July 4 since the cane needed attention at that time. When the stalks were mature, we then had to yank the long thin leaves, called fodder, from the stalks. The heavy tassels of seed at the top of each stalk would shake causing the tiny seeds to fall down on our heads and necklines. Consequently, we had to wear wide brim hats and perhaps a neckerchief to avoid those seeds. This was worse than picking cotton; at least, we could lie down on our half-filled cotton sacks

The picture above was taken one night as we enjoyed a pancake social at our syrup mill. Several people I remember (L to R) R.C. and Wynelle Hammonds, Rastus Puckett is playing the banjo and my little brother, Ken, is watching Rastus! Sitting on a bench is Buell Wilkes and Mary Kellett is standing at the far right. One of the large syrup pans is also visible.

and daydream! Later on, Daddy and his agronomist friends from Auburn decided it would be all right to leave the fodder on the stalks, thank goodness. This was cause for celebration for the Cobb children.

In addition to raising sorghum cane, we also grew cotton. When the plants grew two to three inches in height, we had to chop the weeds away to insure the plants would grow and produce healthy cotton bolls, which would eventually blossom into fluffy cotton. During the spring while the cotton plants were maturing, my brother and I secretly pulled many of the hard green bolls from the plants for two reasons: one, we needed them for use as hand grenades when we played "war," and secondly, we surmised the fewer the bolls remaining, the less cotton we would have to pick later in the summer. Eventually, our dad reprimanded us for this behavior as he did our two older sisters because of their "peanut caper." They obviously tired of helping plant the tiny peanuts by hand, and tossed a container of the peanuts in a nearby ditch to expedite their work.

They told Daddy they finished early! No one knew of this discrepancy until springtime when my father found peanut vines growing profusely in a nearby ditch!

This picture is of my dear friend and former Sand Mountain neighbor, Colene Wilkes, as a young girl, enjoying the juice from a stalk of sorghum cane.

9

MY AUNT VOLA

From an early age, I had dreams, plans, and goals of what I wanted to do with my life though I had no one in my immediate family with whom I was comfortable in sharing them. My two older sisters were always busy in their own areas of interests and activities; however, my Aunt Vola, seemed to be interested in all I did and I loved her dearly. She was my role model and I loved the time I spent with her. I watched her play the piano and taught myself to play based on those observations. Vola's worn Bible was always nearby and when I spent the night at her house, she always kissed me goodnight on my forehead and told me she loved me.

**Vola and
Bonnie, 1993**

Vola was creative. She used a little wood burning set to make a wooden plaque to place above her kitchen windows. The plaque had the following words burned into the wood, "Give Us This Day Our Daily Bread," and I always felt peaceful in her kitchen. When her son, Franklin, was born she let me help care for him. He would sit in his high chair and I would feed him Cheerios, one at a time! I enjoyed helping her as we washed the dishes. All these memories I greatly cherish. Are you a role model for anyone?

Because there were few girls my age living nearby, I was often lonely in our big family. My two sisters could visit cousins their age at our Aunt Myrtle's home and my brother could also go there because there were boy cousins his age; however, I was not allowed to go, so the only place I really felt peaceful and loved as a young girl was when I visited Vola, who lived about a mile from our house. My mother worked diligently to make a better life for our family and she had little time to just sit down and visit. My two older sisters did everything together with Mary taking the lead as Jackie was more passive. They were even roommates in college. I came along five years later and then my little brother was born two years after that ~ finally, the son our parents always wanted!

And so, I was quite talkative, inquisitive, and always asking questions. My parents never said, "Shut Up!" for which I'm grateful; however, it was obvious that of the four children, I was the talker and soon I began to feel I had been a disappointment ~ too tall, too talkative, should have been a boy ~ have YOU ever felt similar disappointments? Knowing Jesus will be your best friend is the key to happiness!

I often felt lonely but I had a vivid imagination and my visits to Vola's were my salvation. Since she had no children for some time, I looked forward to our discussions and I felt she loved me as her own. I cherish those memories and still have many letters she wrote me through the years before her death several years ago.

Vola was my biggest role model at an impressionable time in my life. After I married and had children, I always took my latest pictures to show her when I visited. She was very interested in my activities and asked many questions about events in my life. She taught me how to reach out to others and make them feel special, by her actions toward me. Almost all her letters ended with "Go for it, Bonnie!" Are YOU making a difference in anyone else's life today? It takes so little to be above average!

When I was ten years old, I came to realize there were three things I yearned for in my life:

❖ Someone to kiss me on the forehead and say, "I love you, Bonnie," because my parents worked so hard they hardly had time to do such a thing. People weren't as demonstrative back then as they are today. Yet, I longed for that affirmation.

❖ I wanted to have my own clothes, not just hand-me-downs from my sisters. Because I was tall, the waist on my hand-me-downs clothes was always too big and Mother would simply pin the loose fabric together with vigor.

❖ I wanted to live in town rather than working on a farm. My brother and I spent hours daydreaming about living in the city, especially where there was no cotton or sorghum cane to harvest.

When we realize what it is that we want or need, we are on the first steps to reaching those desires in the future if we persist. And so,

❖ I came to realize that God loved me. He didn't care how tall or talkative I was. He loved me just the way I was.

❖ Secondly, I learned to sew when I took home economics in high school, so I sewed most of my own clothes for years and they always fit nicely!

❖ And, living in the city has happened. I hasten to add that I have many fond memories of Sand Mountain and the wonderful people there. And, I am still in touch with many of my dear friends and family today. Sand Mountain is where I learned to find...

"Happiness On A Shoestring!"

10

My Dad,
Vernal T. Cobb

The DeKalb County Agent, Mr. John Pate, and our dad were good friends. Through the Alabama Farm Bureau, Mr. Pate advised farmers on ways to develop farm acreage properly to insure maximum growth, planting kudzu to prevent soil erosion, new ways to properly landscape one's yard, along with many other subjects. The community greatly benefitted from this organization. Mr. Pate's office was in nearby Fort Payne, home of the future country music group, "Alabama!"

My father, V. T. Cobb, was one of the original nine incorporators of the Marshall-DeKalb County Electric Cooperative in northern Alabama on February 28, 1942. This was the beginning of a new way of life for thousands of families in the rural area of Sand Mountain, the area where I was born. In fact, Daddy wired many homes on Sand Mountain with electricity (including ours) and was always talking about the TVA (Tennessee Valley Authority) and the TVA dam near

Guntersville, AL. And of course, his creativity in producing quality sorghum syrup was his trademark in life.

The following article tells of the history. According to a February 1990 newspaper article by Mr. Jesse Culp, Director of public relations of the CO-OP:

"....*These nine individuals were all men of vision, highly regarded, and sincerely concerned about the fact that most families out in the rural areas were not being provided electricity by the Alabama Power Company, the sole provider of electricity in the area.*

These men put together a new cooperative set out to build and energize rural lines. But it was a slow go, because World War II had begun and materials and labor were scarce. However, they did the best they could to keep service going until the war ended. And as soon as materials were again available, a massive program of building was begun which lasted until the early 1950s, by which time virtually every household and business in the area was being served."

Mr. Culp then ended his article by stating, "My hat is off to these pioneers and to all who have followed them in building and maintaining such a fine electrical distribution system as Marshall-DeKalb Electric Cooperative now has, it is one of the most dependable and efficient in the land!"

I still remember the evenings my dad attended those co-op meetings. Daddy was tall and handsome.

**Tisha and
Vernal Cobb 1979
Bonnie's Parents**

He was a good listener, a diplomat, and possessed a deliberate manner which I admired immensely. He was good at making long range plans and executing them. He was even-tempered, he had an incredible sense for understanding people and was respected by his peers. Looking back, I can see he led an exemplary life. He and Mother made a good team. They spent most of their waking hours working, but drew great satisfaction from their efforts. They both enjoyed music and passed that love on to all their family.

Sand Mountain Sorghum

Many people said that my dad made the best sorghum syrup in the country. I wrote and sang some commercial jingles for our syrup business which were aired on local radio stations on Sand Mountain during the syrup season. The following was my Mother's favorite radio commercial which I sang to the tune of "Sugar in the Morning," with a Lady Bird Johnson accent, as follows:

> Sorghum in the Evening,
>
> Sorghum at Suppertime.
>
> Eat a little Sorghum,
>
> on Biscuits it's just Fine.
>
> Pour it on Waffles;
>
> Pour it on Pancakes,
>
> Pour it on Candied Yams,
>
> Eat a little Sorghum ~
>
> It's mighty good, Yes Mam!
>
> - Bonnie Skinner

Cobb's Sorghum Mill, Boaz, AL

One sunny day, Ken and I were playing near one of the big syrup vats and he accidentally caused a large vat lid to shift just enough that he fell into the half cooked juice. Fortunately, it was not hot and as he was being retrieved people began laughing. It made me furious; however, I was glad they found my little brother in that dark sticky liquid. It's no wonder he's so sweet!

Tisha and V.T. Cobb, Bonnie's Parents
testing their sorghum syrup

11

Jacksonville, Alabama

Because of failing health, my parents could no longer operate the farm so it was sold. We moved to Jacksonville, Alabama, where I graduated from high school and college, both on the same campus. My two older sisters had also graduated from that college as well.

My brother, Ken, and I missed our friends on Sand Mountain but we quickly became acclimated to our new environment. Ken joined the high school band and later the college band as well. We especially enjoyed the community swimming pool down the street on West Francis Avenue. This was my first opportunity to practice my Esther Williams swimming skills since I had never been in a pool. I must confess: I did practice in my bedroom every night in front of a mirror when we lived on Sand Mountain! Esther was my favorite actress and I still have copies of all her movies. I quickly discovered the importance of holding one's breath while swimming and smiling under water as Esther did in all her great movies ~ it was much more difficult than I had anticipated!

While I was sorry to leave my friends behind, I was excited to live in the city where there were sidewalks, a telephone, and knowing I could walk to the movies. I missed my girlfriends at Crossville High School ~ Frances, Frankie, Betty and Vivian, and my special friend, Buell. My brother quickly found a buddy with whom he could trade comic books, which was the norm back in those days. Moving in March of 1947 was good because we made new friends before the end of the school year.

I have to tell this story! Moving from the country was more difficult for Mother than we realized. She insisted on bringing our cow, "Bossy," to Jacksonville. "Bossy" lived in a little barn at the back of our property. Every day we had to walk that cow across the street and down a path leading to a large pasture behind the houses on the opposite side of our street. I could envision having a lovely horse for these walks; but, leading a COW across our street and to the pasture was cause for terrible embarrassment as far as I was concerned. When this chore was mine, I made sure the cow was rushed across that street and out of sight as fast as possible. I felt this was something that Heidi might do in the Alps, but not me in Jacksonville! My daily goal was to get that cow out of sight ASAP! Unfortunately, such was not always the case.

One summer day, old "Bossy" escaped and we couldn't find her anywhere. I was so afraid she went to the high school looking for ME! We later found her clop-clopping down West Francis Avenue as if she owned the neighborhood! My goal at that moment was to get that cow back in the little barn as quickly as possible because of the clop-clop noise she was making. I was so afraid some of my friends would see her. Finally, we successfully led the cow back to the barn for the night. I often wondered what the neighbors thought when they heard the sound of that cow's hoofs walking down the street, though I never asked! I was relieved that "Bossy" also left town when our parents moved back to Sand Mountain a couple of years later. This was a stressful time for me in many ways. Little did I realize that being seen with a cow was the least of my problems.

On a sad note, our parents were both experiencing various health issues during these years and life was difficult for Ken and me. Our oldest sister, Mary, had a take-charge personality while our other sister, Jackie, was easy going. Mother had often relied on Mary's judgment for running the household through the years, which was stressful for all concerned, including Mary. After graduating from college, Mary was married and moved away. Mother was simply too distraught to attend the wedding which was a very sad time. She basically became incapacitated due to her maniac depressive symptoms and menopausal condition stemming from the fact she has "lost" her support system. This was before medication was available for such illnesses. Our other sister, Jackie, also graduated from college a short time later, married and moved away as well. During the following three years, Ken and I fended for ourselves. Most of the household chores fell on my shoulders during this period.

The next couple of years were traumatic due to Mother's problems and the fact our Dad seemed to miss his Sand Mountain connections. His health had waned somewhat and he eventually required corrective surgery for a botched appendectomy of many years before. Neither of our parents were in very good health during this time, so Ken and I forged ahead as best as possible. I was proud of my brother as he became very active in the high school band and Civil Air Patrol.

My dad bought an appliance store in Jacksonville which also included a record department and bus station. I helped him as much as possible, primarily by working in the record department. I worked after school and part time on Saturdays for my dad. I accumulated a great collection of favorite songs (78 rpm) of that era in lieu of a meager salary. I enjoyed getting acquainted with all genres of music and making new friends. It was fun to share music titles and artists with high school and college friends as well. My dad reported to me that we made enough money in "my department" to cover operating expenses for the entire business. However, Mother also needed my help in our kitchen and other home chores. She was in bed most of the time and I barely had time to study. Many of the chores and responsibilities fell on my shoulders and this was the most stressful time of my life. I was hesitant to bring friends home because I never knew how Mother would be feeling, so it was easier to simply avoid the situation.

On a lighter side, my best friend in Jacksonville became Phyllis Rice. She lived down the street and we shared many common interests. She played the piano beautifully and we enjoyed visiting each other and singing all the songs from our respective collections of sheet music. We also sang in the church choir during this time and attended various church functions. We continue to remain good friends even though we now live in different cities.

During my senior year of high school, I was thrilled to be voted Homecoming Queen, which to me was amazing even though my parents were not at the event. My escort was Bill Weaver who lived in Jacksonville. Since there was no high school youth programs in our church, I participated in the college Wesley Foundation which our church sponsored. My friend, Phyllis, and I enjoyed many events associated with Wesley throughout our senior year in high school and college as well. We attended church retreats and still enjoy many fond memories of those days. I appreciated getting away from my chores and being with students in a friendly environment.

A special treat we high school girls enjoyed was getting our photographs taken by Olan Mills when their representative came to town. We styled our hair as best as possible (no hair dryers at that time) and then rushed to the studio to have our photo taken ~ an eight by ten photo for only one dollar. This was always a fun thing to do in the late forties.

President
Harry S. Truman
Photo taken by
Bonnie

The highlight of my high school senior year was when our class of about eighty students made a memorable two-week trip to Washington, DC, and New York City in the spring of 1948. We sold magazine subscriptions to help defray expenses for the trip. As our two buses neared Washington, DC, in the evening it was a memorable sight: the city was bathed in spotlights shining on the massive buildings and magnificent monuments. I thought to myself: I would like to live here someday. That trip made a lasting impact on my life which I will share later. Our class attended a Presidential function in the Rose Garden at the White House where President Harry S. Truman spoke.

We continued our journey on to New York City where we saw Ethel Merman in a great Broadway play, "Annie Get Your Gun." This was much more exciting than any of my housetop memories on Sand Mountain! (Even when I pretended to be the "Sorghum Princess" as I sat on our rooftop and waved to passersby!)

A humorous thing happened in New York City which I still enjoy recalling. One morning two other girls and I decided to eat breakfast across the street from our hotel. Naturally, we were excited to be in "downtown New York City" alone for a very brief time. As we were paying our bill the man at the cash register said, "What part of the South are you girls from?" I innocently remarked, "What makes you think we're from the South?" He remarked, "Honey, it's written all over your faces!" He probably heard our accents as well! That 1948 senior trip was a great experience and changed my life forever.

College began for me in the fall of 1948; however, there was little excitement in our household about my plans. Mother continued to experience serious health problems and the situation was more of a role reversal. Since I did not have a college wardrobe, I continued wearing my high school clothes and often did not have time to study properly. I walked to the campus alone and registered without fanfare. My dad wasn't feeling well either and in addition, he was occupied with the operation of the appliance store. I spent most of my free time helping him.

I wanted to live in the dormitory as my sisters had; however, our home was within minutes of the campus, so I lived at home. I stayed busy with household chores, college classes, working part time as secretary to the Registrar and also helping my father in his store after school. On Saturday mornings, I typed the church bulletins for two churches using the old-fashioned mimeograph machine. For this I was paid fifty cents weekly by each church. This was indeed a difficult and busy time for me.

Fortunately, my parents moved back to Sand Mountain before my senior year of college began, so I was finally able to move into the college dorm for a very short time. As much as I enjoyed college and loved my family, my home life during this period had been very stressful. I couldn't have friends over because I was never sure what the situation would be due to Mother's health at that time.

It was a wonderful day when I moved into the dorm, Daughette Hall. I loved dorm life and was thankful I finally lived on campus if only for a short time. On Sunday nights, I earned a little money by collecting clothing of dorm residents for dry cleaning. My best friend, Phyllis, and I shared a dorm room since her parents had also moved back to their original home as well. As a college music major, Phyllis was always involved in musical events and played the piano beautifully. By attending college during the summer months, both Phyllis and I graduated from college in three years. She and her husband, Tom, now live in Decatur, Alabama, and we remain in touch even today.

Throughout my college days, I continued working in the Registrar's Office every hour I was not in class. I was an excellent typing and shorthand student and that job fit my abilities perfectly. I never saw any of the money I earned as I merely walked down to the Treasurer's Office at the end of each month, turned in the number of hours I worked and that paid all of my tuition. I did not have any "spending money" but in those days, everyone was basically in the same situation. We all lived on a shoestring.

As a college sophomore, I was fortunate in being asked to represent DeKalb County, in the upcoming "Alabama Maid of Cotton" pageant to be held in Birmingham. I wasn't particularly fond of the title because my brother and I had detested picking cotton; however, this afforded me an opportunity to go to Birmingham to the glorious Tutwiler Hotel for the pageant. I did not win the state title, but I did get my picture in the Bir-

Bonnie in Cotton Field

mingham News, which to me was just as exciting. Back on the campus the following Monday morning, someone handed me the paper saying, "Bonnie, your picture is in the paper!" I sauntered over ~ feeling pretty impressed until I read a line underneath the picture which changed my life. It said, "Bonnie grew up on Sand Mountain and has picked cotton all her life!" – drats! I thought this would be the end of me; however, that was a good lesson for me to always remember and today, I'm still proud of my heritage!

In my junior year of college, I was honored to be elected the Homecoming Queen and this was indeed a special thrill for me. My good friend, Jimmy Gamble, was my escort. He carried my hat after I was crowned and we had a great time. The memorable Homecoming Parade down Pelham Road in Jacksonville reminded me of the times I sat on our Sand Mountain rooftop waving to the passing cars. I loved waving to friends en route during that parade!

Our college had five annual formal college dances each year with the big band sound and lots of jitterbugging. I have many fond memories of helping decorate the gym, finding an appropriate dress to wear, receiving corsages (preferably one of gardenias), and lots of dancing. One of our music majors in college, Johnny

Long, had a great band during this time and was a favorite at our dances. I remember that band leader, Harry James, brought his band to Jacksonville for one of our big dances.

Another honor I received was that of being named "Miss Ideal Secretary" which was nice and an affirmation that I was in the appropriate major in college. I also belonged to the Citizenship Forum where we learned more about government procedures. As a delegate to a National Citizenship Conference in Washington, DC, along with three other students, I was fortunate to meet one of our Alabama United States Senators at the capitol, Honorable John J. Sparkman. Little did I realize that in a short two years I would be working in his Washington, DC, office! I knew I had been blessed and thanked God every day for all these blessings.

As a senior in college, I was pleased to accept a job as secretary to our college president, Dr Houston Cole, upon graduation; however, he and Senator Sparkman were good friends and he released me from our agreement when he learned of Senator Sparkman's offer. All this sounds glamorous and exciting; but first, I must tell you about our "shoestring" departure from Alabama to travel to our Nation's Capitol.

A few days after college graduation, my parents drove me to Washington, DC. They were now living in Geraldine, Alabama. My brother, Ken, then a high school senior, also made the trip which was reminiscent of our shoestring trip to Tampa, Florida, many years earlier which I have mentioned (this trip was made without the infamous nail keg, however!). And, this time, we had a car to replace the truck. Daddy had bought a maroon

Kaiser '49 and the car was now loaded with all my worldly possessions, including my stack of cherished 78 rpm records, a little blue record player, and six new dresses from Sears.

We drove straight from Geraldine, Alabama, to Washington, DC, making pit stops only for gasoline and nature. My dear father was most comfortable in overalls but I assumed he would not be wearing them on this trip. We departed Geraldine at "O-Dark-Thirty" in the morning. It was only after the sun had risen that I looked over and noticed Daddy happily wearing his favorite overalls as we headed toward our nation's Capitol! "I'll change later," he promised! OMYGOSH!

We ate the customary crackers, cheese and oranges en route along with a new addition to our menu, Vienna Sausage, complete with a key to unwind the little metal strip around the top edge for easy opening. And, we had a jar of water (this was before bottled water!).

Daddy announced that we were driving straight through to DC, so I easily envisioned the four of us standing on the Capitol steps with all my belongings, completely disheveled, with unmatched luggage, an empty water jar, and Daddy in his overalls. It was not my intention to arrive in MY new city in this fashion!

Daddy kept saying he would stop at the next service station and change his pants; however, before he realized it, we had crossed a river and there we were ~ in downtown Washington, DC! Fortunately, we found a service station and he managed to change into trousers a short time later. We located my apartment and I felt a great sigh of relief.

Looking back, things were not always as we would have liked; however, in spite of the difficulties, it was good to know our parents did the best possible for us at any given time. I also realized that not many young ladies had such an opportunity as I was about to experience in Washington, DC. At the age of twenty, I quickly learned to appreciate the things I did have and the new adventures that were about to come my way. I gladly accepted the responsibilities for my future happiness and felt blessed that I had reached a new direction in my life.

For example, I'm glad I learned to sew and "make do" at an early age, because my shoestring life continued for many years ahead!

12

Washington, DC

Once I settled into my apartment, became acquainted with my three new roommates and began my new job, I felt quite at home. Working for Senator Sparkman was more than I ever dreamed it would be ~ even when I sat in my upstairs window at Freeman singing, "It Might As Well Be Spring"! I was finally "Somewhere Else.... Walking Down a Strange New Street"!

I quickly found my niche in a wonderful church on Sixteenth Street, joined the choir and immediately became involved in activities which kept me happily occupied. I missed my family and friends, but this was exactly what I longed for all my life ~ opportunities for growth and a chance to see a bigger picture of life.

Living in Washington, DC, was a remarkable experience. The Senate Office Building, where I worked, was diagonally across the street from our nation's Capitol. Each secretary in our office alternated working late. The Senator was often on the Senate Floor and unavailable to come to the office to dictate letters. Therefore, we had to be available to meet his requirements.

My first week began in an amazing manner. During this time, our President was Harry S. Truman. I learned that Vice President Alben Barkley's office was nearby and I often saw him in the hall. Mrs. Harry S. Truman (Bess) came to the Senate Office Building for Red Cross Meetings and I couldn't believe I was standing nearby! And a popular movie star at that time, Van Johnson, was being filmed in a movie over in the Capitol Rotunda which I often observed during my lunch hours. There were special seats in the Senate Gallery for office personnel and I spent most of my lunch hours simply sitting there observing the procedures and learning the names of all the Senators. And, I enjoyed the Senate Bean Soup which was regularly served, by law, in the Senate Dining Room.

My first Tuesday to work late was my second week on the job. Everyone in the office had left for the day and I was alone, on Capitol Hill, my second week in Washington, DC. Suddenly, the phone rang and a man's deep voice said, "Bonnie, are there any calls for me?" Not recognizing the voice, I said, "May I ask who is calling?" He said, "This is the Senator!" What a way to begin my career on Capitol Hill!

He was very nice and asked me to bring the dictation over to the Capitol since he couldn't leave the Senate Floor because of an upcoming vote. So, I took the Senate Subway over to the Capitol with my box of work, rode an elevator up to the Senate Floor and entered the majestic double doors leading into the Senators' Lounge. I looked through some glass panels on more double doors leading directly out onto the Senate Floor where I could see all the Senators at work. In the lounge I saw a long table lined with newspapers from every state, neatly arranged alphabetically, waiting for the Senators to read when time permitted. I sat down in a plush chair by a window while I waited for Senator Sparkman to come from the Senate Floor. As I looked out one of the west windows, I had a perfect view of the entire Washington Mall, including the tall Washington Monument which I had walked down with other high school seniors in 1948! The year was 1951 and I have always felt so blessed to have had such an amazing opportunity in my short twenty years of life.

Other memorable events in DC included seeing many famous celebrities during that time as they often made appearances between movie features in local theatres ~ Patti Page, Johnny Ray, Tony Curtis, Janet Leigh, and The Four Aces (one of the first musical groups of that time), and others. I attended an Army-Navy football game in Philadelphia with free tickets from a constituent in our office and I attended a Billy Graham Crusade when he was just beginning his amazing ministry. Every Sunday after church, my three roommates and I went sightseeing with other friends. I enjoyed taking pictures of the beautiful cherry blossoms along the Potomac River in the spring. I have nothing but fond memories of my time in Washington, DC, and wish every high school senior could enjoy a trip to DC, as I did back in 1948.

I was active in my new church, Foundry Methodist Church. Our pastor, Dr Harris, was also the Chaplain of the U.S. Senate at that time. I enjoyed singing in the large church choir. Our choir was exceptional and we were invited to sing for various programs across the city and were paid to do so. My most memorable event with the choir was when we sang with the United States

Marine Band at a National Chamber of Commerce Convention in the DAR Building.

I quickly learned to be happy ~ there were so many things to do and see without spending any money. This was indeed "Happiness on A Shoestring" at its best!

Congress typically adjourns in the fall in Washington, DC. The Congressmen return to their respective states, open a temporary office, and serve the constituents in a more personable manner. Two other secretaries and I were designated to return to Alabama with Senator Sparkman to open a local office for a few weeks in Huntsville, Alabama, the home of Senator and Mrs. Sparkman. We three secretaries alternated serving as receptionist at the front desk while the other two received dictation and typed letters in the back office.

It was my first day to work out front as the receptionist. I was doing a good job until a shabbily dressed man with a strange accent came in wanting to see the Senator. I asked him for his name twice and still could not understand anything he said. Finally, I asked him to write down his name, which he did, and I took it into Senator Sparkman's office and told him the story. He glanced at it and said,"My goodness, Bonnie, that's Werner Von Braun, the noted German rocket scientist! Show him in quickly!" This was in 1951! I wish I had kept that signature!

Working in the Senator's Office was an awesome experience and something I shall remember always. In fact, had my father not been able to attend my wedding later on in Washington, DC, Senator Sparkman agreed to stand in as my Dad. He was a decent, honorable man.

I have always tried to think and plan ahead. With that in mind, my new long term goal at that time was to save my money for an educational tour of Europe in the future and possibly work overseas with the State Department. I also stayed busy with extra curricular activities and continued to grow in all areas. My wish for college age people today would be that each one could spend a year in our nation's Capitol.

13

2nd Lt. and Mrs. Jack Skinner

The following year, I was refreshment chairman for a singles program in my church in Washington, DC, and I also worked in the church kitchen once a month helping serve free meals to servicemen. One spring evening I served a plate of spaghetti to a handsome cadet attending Army Officers Candidate School (OCS) who came with some buddies from Fort Belvoir, VA, for a free meal. Somehow, he eventually convinced me to alter my career plans! We were married later that year. My frugal childhood paid off: I had already saved enough money from my job by then to pay for our wedding and help Jack pay for his new officer's uniforms ~ now, that's really what "Happiness on A Shoestring" is all about!

We had a lovely, but simple, chapel wedding at my church with a reception at the home of my church friends, Colonel and Mrs. Gattis. My best friend, Phyllis, was now working in Washington, DC, and she was my Maid of Honor. And, my dad gave me away.

My Alabama parents and Jack's Colorado relatives enjoyed this occasion to become acquainted. My dear landlady, Mrs. Jardeleza, baked a beautiful wedding cake for the reception. And so, the "Shoestring" theme continued!

My grandmother, (Mama, the one from Tampa, Florida, whom I've mentioned earlier) accompanied my parents to Washington, DC, but her greatest desire was to see where President Lincoln was assassinated and then, to go to the Washington, DC, Zoo, with our wedding being secondary on her agenda! I had planned to have a day of rest on my wedding day; however, Mama's agenda superseded all else! Now, it's always dreadfully hot and humid in DC in

2nd Lt. and Mrs. Jack Skinner
June 26, 1952

June and we had no air conditioning in our apartment at that time; however, President Lincoln would have been very proud of me ~ we spent most of the day at the Ford Theatre and across the street where Lincoln actually died. And, the entire wedding party enjoyed being at the Zoo the rest of the day as well. Our wedding was at 5:30 PM and we basically had to rush to the church to meet the preacher!

The following day Jack and I departed Washington, DC, for our new home in Rolla, Missouri, near Fort Leonard Wood, for his first military assignment as a 2nd Lieutenant.

We located an apartment (actually a reconstructed loft), and even though the ceilings slanted quite a bit, we enjoyed our first home. Basically, we had to lower our heads to get in bed because of the slanted ceilings. This was an omen of things to come when we later lived in a Quonset Hut which also had slanted ceilings throughout

The outside stairs leading to our apartment were great for exercise and there was a clothes line in back to hang out the laundry. With my first load of laundry, I lovingly hung each piece carefully on the line. When I went out to bring in the dried clothes, I was shocked to see black soot scattered on our new white sheets and Jack's white underwear ~ I was distraught!

Our first
home

I soon learned the air carried soot from other wood burning stoves in this semi-rural area and this fre-quently happened, and this was before clothes dryers. As soon as my next load of laundry seemed dry,

I quickly brought it back into our apartment. From my three small recipe books I enjoyed preparing "shoestring meals" and waiting for my new husband to return from the base. Such was our new life in Rolla, Missouri.

During our stay in Missouri, we became good friends with the Coffmans and Juilfs. We played lots of canasta and enjoyed making French fries which was the most economical snack of the day. Also, we enjoyed fishing in the Merrimac River and I remember seeing water cress for the first time growing profusely in the streams of ice cold water.

On a silly note, Jack and I had a hilarious time engaging in a water battle one day in our small apartment! It started when we were sitting on the bed facing each other while playing canasta. There was a fun disagreement about a card that was played and Jack said, "If you do that I'll tear this card in half." Then I said, "If you tear that card, I'll spit on you!" Before we knew what happened, we were chasing each other around our small apartment, bumping our heads because of the low ceiling. All this somehow turned into a water battle; however, I rushed into the bath room and locked the door feeling safe and snug. Jack rushed down those outside back stairs, grabbed the water hose and put it through the tiny bathroom window by the door and you-know-who was drenched! This sounds silly now, but it proves the fun of young love and the fact that people can have fun on a shoestring!

Several months later, Jack and his boss, Major Lewis, went rabbit hunting. Don't ask me for details ~ this was a long time ago! Anyway, they came home later that day with some dressed rabbits and I had never cooked a rabbit! Major Lewis assured us that we could have all the rabbit meat which they had cleaned and sectioned before coming home. So I dutifully told Jack I would be happy to fry this "delicacy" for him. I surmised the way to prepare this was to treat it like fried chicken. As the rabbit was frying, the acrid odor took me aback and I became deathly nauseous. In fact, Jack had to eventually call a doctor who came to our apartment and gave me a shot to ease the nausea! It was also the beginning of the realization that I might be pregnant! My advice to any new bride: avoid cooking rabbit under any circumstances!

Later when we learned that Jack's next assignment would be in Germany, we decided my living in Alabama would be the best choice for that time, because I was indeed pregnant. We found a nice room in a home near my sister, Jackie, and her husband in Anniston, Alabama. We were also a short distance from my alma mater, Jacksonville State University, as well as the military hospital at Fort McClellan. Jackie and I had a memorable time being together again and I spent many hours with her enjoying their new daughter, Nancy, my first niece. I also enjoyed seeing many of my college friends who lived in the area.

When our son, David, was born at the military hospital at nearby Fort McClellan, both our mothers came to "care for me". Jack's mom came from Denver and Mother came down from Geraldine, Alabama. They were sorry I was "alone" and wanted to help. Since Jack's Mom was a nurse, I felt privileged to have her expertise available. Well, as much as I loved them both, they were helpless as far as "help" was concerned! They both wanted to go sightseeing and when it was meal time, neither of them had a clue as to how to prepare the simple prepared frozen meals in my fridge! Also, Jack's Mom slept with me and snored so loudly the bed springs vibrated! Mother stayed with my sister, Jackie, a few blocks away. After about four days, I was ready for them both to leave so I could rest! The only thing Mother enjoyed doing was hanging the diapers out to dry! "It brings back memories!" she said.

However, good news prevailed! One of my college friends told me that my former boss, Senator Sparkman, was scheduled to speak on our college campus the following day! Even though David was only ten days old, I took him AND both mothers up to the nearby campus because I felt I deserved a special treat! I was glad I still had our car available.

Senator Sparkman recognized me in the audience and we had a nice reunion afterwards. He enjoyed seeing my new son and many photographs were taken.

Senator Sparkman, David and Bonnie (Jack's mom in back)

Here's a word of wisdom for you new moms: Don't let your mothers take care of you unless they promise to let you adequately rest!

David and I arrived in Germany when he was three months old. As I stepped off the plane, I handed our baby to his new father and said, "Jack, It's YOUR turn!"

14

Domesticated Bliss

Thus, my exciting DC career ended as I joined Jack on a military journey which has been full of love and family, adventures, fun, friends, education, shoestring challenges, excitement and many opportunities for both of us to grow and travel as well. We've lived in many areas ~ Germany, Colorado, Ohio, Arizona, Missouri, Texas, Louisiana, New Jersey, and Oklahoma. We have been blessed with many great friends along the way, and have tried to give our best at every location we called home.

My mantra has always been "Bloom Where You're Planted!" and our many moves have certainly provided opportunities to bloom! Some highlights of our lives along the way follow:

As mentioned, we first lived in Missouri where Jack was stationed at Fort Leonard Wood as a new 2nd Lieutenant. From there he was sent to Germany. Our young son, David, was born the following year at Ft McClellan, Alabama, and the total cost for his delivery was $9.95 ~ our very first "Shoestring Baby!" A few months later, David and I joined the new father in Kitzingen, Germany. We had a wonderful German lady who cared for David while I taught school in the American Dependant's School. This was in 1954, not too long after WWII ended. There were still vestiges of debris from the bombings and it was an interesting time to be there.

We spent a memorable Easter weekend in Paris which proved to be a great place for a delayed honeymoon. We enjoyed seeing Paris and, it was there that I spit off the Eiffel Tower! We decided to have a lovely meal as a final splurge in Paris before returning to Germany. We entered a nice restaurant and when the waiter handed me the menu I said, "Merci beaucoup!" And he said, "Ah, Madam speaks fluent French!" My dear husband said, "Those are the only words she knows!" I could have smacked him! We have many fond memories of those days.

We later returned to Golden, Colorado, where Jack continued work on his degree at the Colorado School of Mines. He received $160 per month on the GI Bill. We lived in veteran's housing in an old military barracks, for a great price of $35 per month. My favorite meal to make was hamburger stew. Our daughter, Susan, was born during this time at the Colorado General Hospital in Denver at a college student discount ~ $45! I remember making bookshelves for our apartment using two ammo boxes Jack brought back from Germany; another shoestring opportunity! We dreamed of a more promising future which kept us focused on our goals.

Jack had an opportunity to attend Air Force Flight School, so we lived in several locations as he completed each phase of his training: first in San Antonio, then to Malden, Missouri; next to Del Rio, TX (I was in a water ballet with the Officer's Wives Club at Laughlin AFB and almost drowned trying to do a swan surface dive! I wondered, "Where's Esther Williams when I really need her?!"); our next move was to Williams AFB, AZ, for more flight training; and then, back to Colorado for Jack to complete his college work.

This time we lived in Boulder, CO, where Jack attended the University of Colorado. We lived in one half of a Quonset Hut in "Vetsville" and our rent was $45 a month for veterans. The Quonset Huts were prominent during World War II and served us well for Jack's remaining college days. Our community of friends in the Quonset Huts became close as we were all in the same situation. There was one pay phone outside our front door, so whoever heard that phone ring, answered it and then called out to the recipient! The Colorado snow became part of our lives as well.

Our Quonset Hut and phone booth at left

While we lived in "Vetsville," I trimmed ladies' hair in our neighborhood for twenty-five cents each. Our living room was the size of our 11 x 15 rug, with slanted walls, but we had a cozy environment. For a Christmas party, we managed to fill the living area with about fourteen people. I had to tilt my head to do the dishes and bathe the babies as the ceilings slanted downward on both sides. I made some curtains and added other shoestring ideas and we were quite comfortable for a meager price.

During that time, I developed a fondness for Mr. Goodbars which I fondly called my "frustration candy". One day, my sweet Susan, who was about three, came to me and said, "Mom, may I have some of your 'stration' candy?" as she pointed to the cabinet where I has stashed my secret sweets.....out of the mouths of babes!

With the GI Bill plus Jack's flight pay from the USAF Air National Guard, we managed to get by on yet another shoestring budget. He graduated in 1958 with a Bachelor of Science in Aeronautical Engineering from the University of Colorado.

When Jack graduated, David was five and Susan was three. Following graduation, we packed up all our worldly possessions, which were few, and moved to Cincinnati where Jack worked with General Electric in the jet engine department.

In 1960 our daughter, Becky, was born in Ohio and again, we found a shoestring hospital who delivered her ~ Maryknoll Hospital was just minutes from our home in Cincinnati and our doctor recommended going there rather than driving into the downtown area which was quite a distance from our home. The doctor added that Maryknoll was primarily a home for <u>unwed</u> mothers, but they also accepted paying patients occasionally. I had a nice stay there as the residents (pregnant single moms) served the meals to the paying patients and the experience was pleasant. The cost was not bad ~ $98. Delivering three children for $152.95 was indeed "Happiness On A Shoestring," we all agreed. Our Becky enjoys telling others where she was born!

In 1962 an opportunity arose for Jack to work at NASA in Houston and we moved there in June of that year. Jack had already driven our car down to Houston from Ohio. He had warned us to expect extremely hot and humid weather. It was also hot in Cincinnati as the movers drove away with our household goods. Two-year old Becky and I sat on our luggage, waiting for David and Susan to come home from school so we could leave immediately for the airport. I was exhausted making sure the house was clean while tending Becky.

I was relieved to have our "logistics for moving" now confined to the luggage and three children; however, when I heard the school children coming home I looked out the door and here comes David ~ riding his bike! I had forgotten the bike! We simply gave it to the boy next door and left. I'll never forget my seven year old Susan's remark as we were flying high in the white fluffy clouds toward Houston, she looked up at me and said, "Mom, are we in Heaven?"

We arrived in Houston in the early stages of the space program. We enjoyed getting acquainted with the seven original Mercury astronaut families. Astronaut Gene Cernan and family lived across the street from us upon their arrival in Houston. In fact, I used their pregnant dog, "Venus," as a visual to explain the birds and the bees to our David, who at that time commented, "Uck"! I later worked on a committee to honor the successful completion of the Mercury phase of the NASA program with a farewell party. During that time, Astronaut John Glenn spoke at our church and the children where so thrilled to see our nation's new hero. For a moment I couldn't find our youngest, Becky, who was four at that time. I saw her in line with a church bulletin waiting to get an autograph of John Glenn. I don't think she had any idea what a great thing that was ~ she was simply in line with the other boys and girls! There was a "Welcome to Houston, NASA" extravaganza at the Houston Coliseum soon after our arrival, so we were there for the initial excitement of the space program.

Once our family was settled in their respective lives in Houston, I took art lessons and actually sold several paintings much to my delight. Each Monday I played the piano for the Space Center Rotary Club for seven years earning a little more money. When an astronaut was a guest at the Rotary Club, I always played "Fly Me to the Moon" as he entered the dining room! I took a flower arranging course and later made four floral arrangements for our new church. We alternated using the arrangements each Sunday for economical purposes because the building fund took precedence at that time. Today, I would have used silk flowers but back then, plastic flowers were the rage. Since our church was small, all the members pitched in wherever possible.

Jack and I worked with the high school youth at our church during this time. He taught Sunday School, I coordinated a talent show for the teens and we chaperoned bus trips to various areas. He also earned his MBA attending night classes. I enjoyed playing bridge with a group of NASA wives during this period. We learned how strong the bond was among those wives when there was an accident in the space program.

During these years, my father had resumed making syrup so I wrote and taped some more radio commercials for his business which were regularly played on radio stations on Sand Mountain. He and Mother were both back on track and feeling much better.

We also had an active USAF Reserves Wives Group out at nearby Ellington Air Force Base, which I enjoyed along with volunteering for PTA projects for Becky's school. This was a productive time for all. During these years, I spent much time in parking lots waiting for our three to participate in various activities. David was the Commander of the high school ROTC Drill Team and active in Civil Air Patrol; Susan was on the high school drill team in the band and later a twirler, then the Drum Major. When Becky was in high school she was also a twirler, so I took advantage of this time to read from my current book which I kept in the car for that purpose. I enjoyed watching many outside practices or marching activities and wanted to be there for them more than anything else.

Our next move was to Barksdale AFB in Bossier City, LA, where Jack was a Flight Commander. We thoroughly enjoyed living in that community and I'm still in touch with my friends, Julia and Yvonne. We lived in a little area called Shady Grove and enjoyed the tall pecan trees on all the streets. Our house on Camille Street sat near the end of the base runway and we could easily watch the B-52 planes taking off and landing as well. We attended Noel Church across the Red River in Shreveport and made many lasting friendships there. I did substitute teaching for awhile in Becky's school and then worked full time at a Shreveport bank as secretary to the Credit Manager.

During this time, our David was home for a few days during a college break in the summer, so he and I chaperoned Becky's junior high church group to Dogpatch, USA, in Arkansas, which was fun.

Jack had bought an old van from some friends for sixty five dollars (only the stereo worked!) with the idea of rebuilding the motor. Instead, David spent his summer vacation working on that van in our garage using a Volkswagen Manual borrowed from the local library. Jack basically suggested to David that he carefully label each item he removed from the van in order to have some sense of organization. And, he had given David a maximum dollar amount he could spend on parts in an effort to get that machine running. After about two weeks, David announced he was ready to make a trial run, much to my surprise and fear. To our amazement, he started the engine and drove the van around the block! He ended up driving the van back to Texas A&M University and drove it until graduation! The library manual he borrowed suffered the most from that experience. It was extremely dirty with oily fingerprints, but that was the only casualty!

In 1977 we were transferred back to Texas where Jack flew C-119's and C-130's with the USAF Reserves at Bergstrom AFB, in Austin, TX. I worked for a Realtor as a Closing Coordinator and thoroughly enjoyed the work. I became editor of their Weekly Newsletter and learned much about selling real estate.

Our children were accustomed to their parents always being part of their activities. Looking back, I think this was one of the most important parenting skills to possess ~ our home was always open to our children's friends. We have many fond memories of various events which occurred in our homes through the years, wherever we lived.

Our daughter, Susan, attended Texas A&M and then received a Physical Therapy Degree from the University of Texas at Galveston. Today, we live near Susan and her family in Norman, Oklahoma. We've enjoyed helping car pool grandchildren while Susan completes work on her doctoral dissertation in music. And, we also enjoy attending various musical programs and playing bridge with Susan and husband, Hal.

Our youngest daughter, Becky, graduated from high school in Austin and entered the University of Texas that fall in time to march with the Longhorn Band, where she later graduated. She and her husband, Jeff, now live in Austin where she works for an energy company and attends night classes working on her MBA.

Our son, David, graduated from Texas A&M University and as an Ensign in the Navy, he flew A-7s off aircraft carriers. He returned to civilian life, earned a MBA, and is now a Senior Partner with Edward Jones & Company. He and Cindy live in College Station, Texas.

And at present, we enjoy our eight grandchildren and four great-grandchildren! We are active in our church here in Norman. I continue to be grateful to Florence Littauer for her love, encouragement and all her books on understanding personalities ~ our family

has greatly benefited from this information in numerous ways. For further information, check the
CLASS website which I've included at the end of this
book.

15

Fun With Gloria

Another military transfer in 1978 found us stationed at McGuire AFB, New Jersey. This proved to be one of my favorite places to live because of the close proximity to New York City. We moved into a new home and Jack enjoyed his job, especially flying C-141's around the world. And, it was here that Gloria Sharp and I first met and we are still great friends today!

While our husbands worked at the base, Gloria and I attended the military wives' functions, which included many fun trips into nearby New York City. Fabulous memories include lunches at the Plaza Hotel and Tavern on the Green; seeing several plays, shopping along Fifth Avenue and taking pictures to record our memories. Gloria was the leader of Skylarks, the military wives' choral group of which I was a member. We sang at nursing homes and other functions and had a memorable experience.

During this time Jack and I became good friends with our New Jersey Realtor and he was interested in my work in Austin with a highly successful real estate firm. As a result, I was invited to speak to their next

Realtor's monthly meeting on the success of my previous employer in Austin, JB Goodwin Realtors. That was actually the first major speech of my life and I enjoyed it immensely. I had no idea how that would become part of my life later.

Gloria and I enjoyed many common interests ~ music, sewing, our families, reading, caring for others, shopping, sightseeing, etc. We found ourselves driving from our homes to the base for military functions two or three times a week, so we alternated driving and enjoying our outings. On the way home, we usually stopped at the local Kmart store for various household needs.

One day as we were entering the store, I mentioned to Gloria that I wanted to buy Barbra Streisand's new Christmas album, so I headed to the music department. Gloria went in another direction. As I was searching for the album, I noticed all the records and albums were in complete disarray, so I straightened up the entire music department ~ it took me almost an hour! My experience in high school when I worked in my father's appliance store in the records area certainly became beneficial for this project. I organized the albums according to the types of music and alphabetically by artists, and when I finished, I was very pleased with the work I had done. As we were leaving I paid for my album and looked forward to listening to Barbra sing all the holiday songs when I reached home.

Since Gloria and I visited Kmart practically every Friday, I made it my responsibility to check the music department and make sure everything was still organized as I had left it. Sometimes, I had to get things back in order but all in all, my weekly checkup worked beautifully. With this attitude, I never got bored!

Several months passed and one day Jack came home and announced that we were being transferred to Ohio. My first remark was, "What about my job?" He had no idea I was "working" so, I told him about my Kmart Caper! We still have to move, he surmised.

And so, the next Friday when Gloria and I stopped at Kmart, I went up to the store manager and said, "Sir, you don't know me but I've been working here for almost a year!" He was aghast! I went on to tell him how I couldn't find a Barbra Streisand album some months before and realized everything was a mess, so I just organized everything and since then, I check it each Friday afternoon when I come in ~ he was totally amazed!

The store manager offered me a job but I told him my husband was being transferred (I didn't mention that Jack was a Colonel!) to Ohio and I had to leave and that he would have to find a replacement for me. He was totally overwhelmed and suddenly, my friend Gloria came walking up and I said, "Hey Gloria, where have you been?" She said, "Oh, I was back in the fabric department getting some of the fabrics back in order!" I didn't mention to the manager that Gloria's husband had

just been promoted to a Brigadier General! See how much fun you can have ~ "On A Shoestring"!

Gloria and Bonnie, 1979

16

Youngstown, Ohio

Our new home was in Ohio. Jack was the Base Commander at Youngstown and enjoyed flying A-37's, another new experience for him. We had grandchildren by now and while we enjoyed living in Ohio, we were looking forward to eventually returning to Texas to be near our family. Sadly, during our stay in Ohio both our fathers died within a short time of each other.

Mother came to live with us. This proved to be a special time for the three of us. One weekend, we took her to Niagara Falls. We rode on the sightseeing boat, "Maid of the Mist," and it was a joy to see Mother let the chilly water splash on her face and glasses. We were wearing the famous bright yellow rain coats. I encouraged her to face away from the mist but she said, "I don't want to miss anything!" I was so thrilled to know she was enjoying this time of her life. She had always worked extremely hard throughout her life and it was a joy to have an opportunity to see her experience many happy days during this period Cof her waning years.

Also, we lived in an area where there was a popular stretch of great restaurants for several miles. Mother and I went out for lunch daily and it was a special treat for both of us. Every day was more special than the last. These are some of my fondest memories of Mother since she was feeling better by this time.

We enjoyed the military base facilities and the people associated with the military program at Youngstown. A memorable faux pau of our Women's Club was when we over-estimated the number of pizzas we could sell when the Air Force Thunderbirds performed at our annual open house. Toward the end of the day we were giving large pizzas to anyone who wanted them! To our relief, they were all gone at the end of the day; however, we did not make as much money as we had anticipated.

This brings to mind another memorable military faux pau which happened in Louisiana when Jack was stationed at Barksdale Air Force Base. Jack called me one day and asked if he might bring some visiting officers over for dinner that night. Now, I prefer a few days' notice, but this was important to Jack and I wanted to please him, so I agreed immediately. He said, by the way, there will be two Colonels and a General. I quickly replied, "No problem!"

Once I hung up the phone, I thought: "Oh, my goodness, what does a General eat?!" And God answered, "The same as everybody else!" I always relied on His word during any emergency but I needed more affirmation that day.

I decided to serve chateaubriand (I hasten to add that this was not in our budget), a nice salad, vegetables, potatoes and cake. After a quick trip to the grocery store, I hurriedly set the table with our best china, crystal and silver and made a quick trip over the carpet with the vacuum. I checked the bathrooms and looked in the mirror and said to myself, "You look pretty good for your age!" This seemed to be something I needed to confirm during this time of uncertainty.

I selected some appropriate music for the evening to enhance the occasion. I was not the least bit nervous, I kept repeating.

It was three o'clock by now, so I decided to prioritize my chores and get busy. First, I made the dessert which was to be a normal, regular cake with delicious frosting; however, after the cake was done, I turned the pan over to place the cake onto a cooling surface. To my utter dismay half the cake stuck to the pan. Omygosh! I quickly spooned the remaining cake out of the pan and surveyed my crumbled mess. I hurriedly put all the cake crumbs into little crystal dessert bowls and made a lemony sauce to cover my mistakes. After adding a mint leaf to the top of each dessert dish for ambiance, I reasoned this would surely suffice, thus avoiding a dessert disaster.

By now, it was four o'clock and I needed to get dressed. I was relieved my potential disaster has been averted. I've always felt if the hostess looks attractive, the meal is just an extra bonus. So I worked on my appearance longer than I should have, let's just put it that way.

The men would be arriving is less than two hours. No problem, everything was running on schedule. I removed the chateaubriand from the fridge to put in the oven for baking, which was to be for a short time according to the recipe book. However, the meat was frozen solid ~ I had inadvertently put it in the freezing compartment rather than the lower area of the fridge when I arrived home from the grocers! What to do? I didn't have time for anything to thaw and this was before microwaves were invented.

However, I had a brilliant idea: why not put the meat in the pressure cooker for a few minutes to simply "loosen up" the process?! After all, I seldom used that cooker and this seemed to be a good time.

As I was getting the pressure cooker out of the cabinet, I was reminded of my own mother's pressure cooker years ago when we lived on Sand Mountain. One day the lady who lived in a little house on our property came up to our house and said, "Mrs. Cobb, I was wondering if I could borrow your 'precious cooker' for awhile today?" Isn't it funny how your mind thinks of such things as this when you're already stressed to the hilt?!

Anyway, the officers arrived and all was well (except the kitchen cook). As the men were enjoying their salads, I was in the kitchen with the pressure cooker hissing and I knew it was time to release all the air so I could slice that meat. How to avoid the noise?! I had not planned this procedure. I covered the cooker with <u>all</u> my pot holders to muffle the sound and I also turned the music to "LOUD". Behold, the pressure cooker hissed and finally fizzled out without the dining guests even knowing of my dilemma!

I had little sweat beads on my brow from my stressful kitchen melee, but I quickly used the pot holders in my hands to wipe my brow and erase all my nervousness!

I served the meat as if we had chateaubriand every night and everyone loved it!

The men agreed ~ the meat was delicious along with the rest of the meal. When I served the dessert, General Bodycombe commented, "Bonnie, this dessert is splendid! What do you call this?" I smiled and replied, "Bonnie Supreme!" He loved it! I learned early on that one does not have to answer a question directly if it is not to their advantage! Now you know the rest of the story.

Let me add that our guests included General Bodycombe, a Colonel Smith, a Colonel Jones and my own Colonel Skinner. My thought was, "To heck with the Colonels, as long as I get General Bodycombe's name correctly, I have it made".

As I was about to offer more coffee, I began to realize I had served a masterpiece dinner, so I kind of relaxed a bit, which was a mistake in retrospect. With my silver coffee carafe in hand, I pranced over to General Bodycombe to offer him more coffee, first because I knew my protocol. After all, he WAS the ranking officer at our table. So, I confidently smiled, tilted my head toward him and said, "Would you like more coffee, General GOODBODY?" Oh dear, why did I say that?!

Realizing my grave error, I simply said, "Sir, don't count on me for Jack's career!" I was totally embarrassed! As it happened, he loved it! And he went back to the Pentagon and told everyone that there was a lady in Louisiana who thought he had a good body ~ who would have thought?!!!

The following year we were at the Hilton Hotel in Washington, DC, attending a Commander's Conference. I was wearing a new boucle red suit in the style of Jacqueline Kennedy and feeling quite patriotic, I must admit. There were several couples in our group who were visiting in the lobby waiting to enter the dining hall for a major luncheon. As we were talking, I noticed the head table personnel crossing the lobby en route to the dining room. Lo and behold, General Bodycombe was leading the group! I turned my back away from the line of distinguished officers hoping he would not recognize me because of my earlier faux pau in Louisiana. I tried to remain as incognito as possible. After all, I didn't want to get my husband fired! As the officers passed our small group, I heard a man's deep voice say, "Is that Bonnie Skinner over there?" I turned around and said, "No, Sir!" He dashed over and said loudly to everyone nearby as he lifted me up: "This lady thinks I have a good body!" I replied, "You still look pretty good!" Oh no, why did I say that?! Poor Jack simply stood there smiling! It's a wonder that he later retired honorably from the military!

We were living in Ohio near the Youngstown Air Base when I received a call from the local TV station requesting I come downtown for an interview on the "Life of an Air Force Wife" or something similar to that.

I agreed to the interview and as I remember, the lady who interviewed me was named Gypsy. She asked many questions about places we had lived, the difficulties in finding the best schools, churches, etc. I was as honest as possible because it is tough to keep all things in perspective when moving as many times as we have. I did request that she stay on the subject and not be impressed with my husband's rank or the opportunities we've had at the various areas, and she agreed. The interview was almost over and I felt good about my comments.

Then Gypsy asked one final question, "One last question, Bonnie, I'd like to ask, is your husband militaristic at home, is he demanding, is it difficult being married to a Colonel?" I couldn't believe she was asking these questions since our interview had gone quite well up to that point, and I had specifically asked her to please not mention Jack's rank in the interview.

Without batting an eye, I responded, "Well, the only difference between Jack and any other man is, he wears his fighter pilot's scarf to bed at night and I have to salute and say, 'Goodnight, Sir!'" I had no idea I would say that! Now, I wondered why I ever agreed to this interview!

As soon as I arrived at home, I called Jack at work and told him the above story. He said he would get back to me shortly. Nervously, I sat at the breakfast table for an hour waiting for him to call me back. The phone finally rang and Jack said he had sent two of the pilots to the TV station to retrieve the tape. The entire staff had watched the interview and then discussed it. I anxiously sat with baited breath and listened to every word and wondered if I would get banned from the base forever! His final comment was, "Everyone loved the tape and voted to keep you!"

17

San Antonio On A Shoestring

Following Jack's retirement from the United States Air Force Reserve, we chose San Antonio as our home, to be near our children and friends as well. We both worked at nearby Kelly Air Force Base in civilian jobs ~ Jack, as an Aeronautical Engineer and I, as secretary to the Command Surgeon at the Electronic Security Command. Yes, I actually had a Top Secret + Clearance!

Because I worked, we ate out often. I sang in the choir of our new church home in San Antonio, we regularly attended programs offered by the San Antonio Symphony as well being members of the San Antonio Knife and Fork Club. We lived across the street from a golf driving range, which Jack enjoyed. We also enjoyed entertaining and traveling for pleasure and yes, we especially were thrilled to be near our children and grandchildren ~ life was great!

Over time we had our home completely upgraded, adding new paint and carpeting. It was nice to finally get things exactly the way we wanted after having moved so many times. And, it was great to have the feeling of being settled after our many moves. And, I enjoyed having a great job with income of my own.

Later, due to failing health, Mother eventually returned to Alabama where she died shortly thereafter. As mentioned before, my older sister, Mary, cared for both parents primarily through the years. After our dad passed away Jack and I were glad to have a chance to help care for Mother for awhile.

On a sad note, however, we lost our dear sister, Jackie, during this time due to diabetic complications. This was a sad loss to our entire family. She had spent some time with us in San Antonio helping to get Mother settled following our move from Ohio and we were looking forward to another visit from her in the near future. We had even located a great nearby apartment for her in case she decided to join us in Texas permanently.

Jack's final military commitments ended and he became a Realtor for several years; he also taught flying at a local flight school, a Community College, and a high school. I continued enjoying my work in the Command Surgeon's Office. We both enjoyed reading and doing meaningful things in our lives. Life just doesn't get any better, we surmised. We had no idea what would happen next.

Our San Antonio Knife and Fork Club met monthly for formal dinners and always had interesting programs. Jack was responsible for the programs one year and I urged him to invite Christian Author and Speaker, Florence Littauer, to speak at one of our dinner meetings. I appreciated her books on understanding one's personality and wanted to meet her. We enjoyed hosting Florence and her husband, Fred, when they came to San Antonio and became acquainted during their visit. Florence and I spent the day together and became great friends. Her presentation was fantastic and from that moment on, my life changed! After reading Florence's books and Dr Kevin Leman's book on the "Birth Order" I became inundated with thoughts, ways, ideas and a desire to follow up on these interesting subjects.

We have been blessed with a wonderful family. I'm sure you will agree, it is not an easy feat raising children. By this time our three children were finishing their college work. So many thoughts come to mind ~ commitment, dedication, determination, unconditional love, the importance of listening, encouragement, disappointments, dealing with successes and failures, family activities, instilling the love of Jesus Christ in the home, the importance of parents who are totally committed to the business of raising children according to their respective personalities, being a good example for them, and being in tune to life instead of wondering what happened.......and the list goes on. Understanding the personalities has helped immensely in encouraging our own children through the years. I was so appreciative to Florence for all those great books she had written which have helped our family so very much. In the near future those books would change my life to a new direction.

As I worked in the Command Surgeon's Office in the late 1980's, many military personnel came in with assorted problems which my boss handled; however, many civilian ladies also came in to visit with me and many seemed to have heavy hearts. They obviously needed someone to simply listen as they shared their woes and I am a good listener. Many of the ladies were divorced and worked out of necessity. As I listened to their stories, I came to realize they basically needed someone to encourage them. I have always enjoyed reading positive, motivational books and I would recommend a book that perhaps had helped me at some time. I loaned many of my own books to these ladies.

Over the course of several months, I had occasion to listen to numerous stories and when appropriate, I offered words of encouragement to these ladies. The military personnel knew when they came in with a question, it would be answered by the Command Surgeon. Except for the Chaplain, there was no one available for civilian women. Therefore, I basically saw myself as that encourager. However, I felt quite comfortable in discussing some of these situations with our base Chaplain. We enjoyed a nice working relationship.

I enjoyed coffee with my friend, Sharon, every morning and we discussed the situation about women needing encouragement and the need for someone to simply listen. We realized most of these people had absolutely no one in whom they could share their concerns.

One day I returned to my desk after a coffee break when the topic of discussion was again how to find ways to help these ladies. I began work on an office project. The discussion I had just had with Sharon was heavy on my heart. After sitting down at the computer, I rested my elbows on my desk, placed my forehead in my hands and quietly said, "Dear God, what can I do to encourage these women and help them know there's more to life?" I went back to work on the office project which was due at the end of that day. I felt I had done all that I could possibly do at that point.

I certainly was not expecting an answer to my little "prayer". However, an entire plan for leading a series of retreats for women was revealed to me in less than three hours that same day. While I was typing on that office project, I did not realize that I had also been jotting down ideas on little post notes and sticking them over my desk top! I later gathered up those notes and prioritized them. To my utter amazement, I had created complete plans for leading three different retreats for these women, and the biggest surprise of all ~ they were to be held in MY OWN HOME! Never before did I have any notion of leading retreats out of my home! Lesson Learned: Be aware of what you pray for!

The plan was simple: There would be three retreats on ways to take care of oneself ~ a retreat on the MIND, the second on the SOUL, and the third on the BODY. I felt this was something I could do. The ladies would arrive no later than 8:00 Friday night for each retreat and leave at 4:00 Saturday afternoon. And, my husband could spend those Friday nights in the Visiting Officers Quarters at nearby Kelly Air Force Base, which was fine with him. When I shared these ideas with Jack, he said, "I think you better do it, Bonnie!"

God had thought of everything, even the title:

"HAPPINESS ON A SHOESTRING"

Happiness on a Shoestring

18

My Shoestring Retreats

I need to add here that I am an ardent reader of the subjects previously mentioned and had many books on ways to enhance one's life, so I felt confident that I could do this even though the idea of leading retreats was never anything I had thought of doing up to this point.

After the plans were made, I distributed flyers to those ladies who had come in to my office to talk with me. I announced my retreat plans and dates. My aim was for everyone to have an enjoyable weekend away from the hustle and bustle of everyday life and to "retreat" in every sense of the word. I wanted them to experience encouragement at a seemingly difficult time in their lives.

The women were asked to bring only a nightie, a tooth brush, a change of clothing and $15 to help defray expenses. By keeping the meals and kitchen activity to a minimum, everyone could concentrate more on the retreat itself. I relied on SAM's for our food. I felt confident God would give me the courage, the wisdom, and the energy to help these ladies have a memorable weekend, and He did!

As you are reading this book, I encourage YOU to think of ways you might be able to make a difference in the lives of others in your own circle of friends and family. What you read, who you meet, what you do in your leisure time ~ all these things and more make you the person you are today. What else can you do? Don't ever rest on your laurels ~ there's always opportunities to grow in some fashion!

With my friend Sharon's encouragement, our first retreat was special in every way. The logistics were simplified: the food from SAM's was great; the ladies slept on couches, beds, or "pallets" on the floor (I put a rose on each pillow as I said a prayer for the woman who would be sleeping there); everyone was treated equally, we used FIRST names only, and no one was allowed to discuss anything work-related, any family members or family concerns. The weekend was simply for each person present and what she was going to do with the rest of her own life! This put everyone on the same level immediately.

Our first retreat was on "The Mind". We played fun games on Friday night. On Saturday morning I gave a synopsis of "The Birth Order," one of my favorite books by Dr. Kevin Leman. I then shared my own birth order and how that affected me as I grew up, and then I asked each of the ladies to do the same. It was incredible! This proved to be a wonderful way to become acquainted because every person has a birth order. We are either the oldest, youngest, middle or only child! And, many come from blended families ~ all this affects how we live our lives. This was a perfect introduction to the weekend because every one of the ladies opened up and talked freely about themselves. The entire morning quickly passed by and it was lunch time before we realized it. Since the rules were not to talk about anyone else or their job, the ladies began opening up and talking freely about their hopes and dreams. This put everyone on the same level or playing field.

After lunch, we had one hour of quiet time. During this hour, each person had an opportunity to study the contents of the colorful folders which I had prepared. One of the projects in the folder was for each person to create a list of their "victories" or positive things that had happened in their entire lives. This list would then be transferred to a journal later where the ladies may continue to include their positive events as they happened. This proved to be a great motivational tool to help others look for good things that happen in their lives and to expect good things in the future.

The remainder of the afternoon of that first retreat was spent studying and understanding the four personality types after reviewing their tests results which revealed each attendee's personality type. The day ended with a great discussion. I've always told my children when you're doing productive things with your life, good things will happen. And, I can certainly attest to that in this case; new horizons were opened for these ladies!

The themes for my other two retreats, the SOUL and the BODY, with similar formats were equally received as well. If you are interested in leading retreats of this kind, I have written a manual with complete details for all three retreats with additional materials for each.

You can reach me by email: b.skinner@cox.net

In addition to the three basic retreats, we have en-joyed several additional activities through the years: the entire group of ladies participated in hosting both bridal and baby showers for some of the ladies; other events to broaden one's horizons; also, there was a sur-prise birthday luncheon for me with forty ladies at-tending. Another event was a bazaar held in my back yard one Saturday. The ladies set up individual booths around our back yard fence to display their arts and crafts. The attendance was fantastic and everyone en-joyed selling their crafts and talents. Each lady paid five dollars to "rent" space for their booth. The money was used to purchase refreshments and to pay for an ad in the paper. It was an amazing day. Many of the women were amazed at the activity that was created among themselves. They learned to bloom where they were planted!

Another event which was special to me was an all-day retreat I planned for a group of black military ladies stationed at the base where I worked. I had met a delightful, attractive black lady at my beauty salon. We discussed the retreats I had been hosting in my home and what I was doing to help women feel good about themselves and she was extremely interested. When I shared my concern about the lack of encourage-ment a group of black ladies at the base must experi-ence since they are required to wear their uniforms daily, with little makeup, I asked her if she would spend the day with us and offer advice on hair, makeup and dress when they are off duty. She was thrilled to par-ticipate. Ten ladies spent the day at my home with my new friend, the hairdresser. She discussed the particu-lar problems associated with the care of their hair;

then she discussed makeup for work and off-duty, as well as proper dress as well.   She brought enough makeup for each girl to learn to apply properly and it was such a joy for me to see all those military ladies sitting on my den floor with their makeup and mirrors, learning new ways to enhance their appearance.   They had a wonderful time and I felt that was one of my best Saturdays ever.

The narrative that follows has always been a favorite of mine and I hope you find it meaningful to you as well:

"You're Special"

You're Special! In all the world there is nobody like you.   Since the beginning of time, there has never been another person like you.

Nobody has your smile.   Nobody has your eyes, your nose, your hair, your hands, your voice.   You're Special.

No one sees things just as you do.   In all of time there has been no one who laughs like you, no one who cries like you do.   And, what makes you laugh and cry will never provoke identical laughter and tears from anybody else, ever.

You are the only one in God's creation with your set of natural abilities.   There will always be somebody who is better at one of the things you're good at but no one in the universe can reach the quality of your combination of talents, ideas, natural abilities and spiritual abilities.

Like a room full of musical instruments, some may excel alone but none can match the symphony sound of the body of Christ when all are played to-gether because God set the members every one of them in the Body as it hath pleased Him.

Through all of eternity no one will ever look, talk, walk, think or do exactly like you. You're Special. You're rare. And, as in all rarity, there is great value. Because of your great value you need not at-tempt to imitate others. You should accept ~ yes, celebrate ~ your differences. You're Special.

Continue to realize it's not an accident that you're special. Continue to see that God created you special for a very special purpose. He called you out and ordained you to a calling that no one else can do as well as you. Out of all the billions of applicants, only one is qualified, only one has the best combina-tion of what it takes. That just as surely as every snow flake that falls has a perfect design and no two designs are the same, so within the Body of Christ also. No two believers are the same and without each member the Body would be lacking and God's plan would be incomplete.

Ask the Father to teach you His divine plan for your life and that it may stand forth revealed for you as it should, unfolding in perfect sequence and perfect order in such a way as to bring the greatest glory to His name. That one is YOU.

Because You're Special!

-Author Unknown

19

A Reservoir
of Information

The following information is a collection of positive, motivational materials which I have collected and utilized in my presentations to the retreats mentioned; also, in speaking across the country. Individuals who attend the CLASS seminars are encouraged to build their own personal collection of these subjects to define their own walk through life. Not only will this be useful as you work on your own presentations or ministries, but we all need constant reassurance and approval as we go through life. Building your own reservoir of information will be of lifetime value in either case.

At my very first retreat, I sat down to rest for a few minutes before the ladies were due to arrive. I had everything ready and as I looked around I could almost sense a darkness next to me on the couch as if someone were saying to me, "What makes you think you can pull this weekend off?" All of a sudden, I began to have doubts and I asked God to give me a sign. I found a pen and paper and begin to write down anything that would come to mind.

I began writing down ONLY positive things that had happened to me in the past that gave me hope, reassurance and confidence. Before long, I had a long list of things that I had done and that encouraged me, some very simple things and other things on different levels. From time to time, I now read these random thoughts just to give myself a lift when I'm feeling rather low. I eventually named this "My Victory Log" and I urge YOU to build your own list of victories and put it in a journal! The greatest advantage of "My Victory Log" is this: when you become sad or depressed, sit down and read some of your own victories and know there's a rainbow at the end of the tunnel. This is a great idea for you to share with your family or friends. Consider this as a way to give yourself a checkup from time to time! If you need some positive motivation or affirmation, chances are you need to get busy! Try to have at least one positive entry each day hence. Never stop adding victories!

I encourage you to get a journal and begin your own "Victory Log" today! In glancing through my own "Victory Log" I now am reminded of some memorable moments, in no particular order, from my own life which I'll share with you below:

❖ I learned to tie my shoes the first day of elementary school! (I still remember thinking, "I wonder what else do I not know?!")

❖ I was president of my ninth grade class.

❖ During the Viet Nam War, I wore the POW bracelet of Brig Gen Robbie Risner until the day that he was released and landed back in the USA. I have had the privilege of knowing both Robbie and Dot since they became members of our San Antonio Church.

He is a wonderful, Godly man, and it was one of my highest honors to wear the bracelet with his name on it during his imprisonment and then becoming friends later.

❖ Back in the 1940's, I was the healthiest 4-H Club girl in DeKalb County, Alabama, in the ninth grade and rode a float in the Inaugural Parade of our new state Governor with my friend, Kermit Hammonds, the healthiest 4-H Club boy.

❖ I made a cornice board for my bedroom during high school days using cardboard covered with fabric.

❖ Walked down the Washington Monument with a group of high school seniors in 1948.

❖ Took a photo of President Truman in the White House Rose Garden on our senior trip in 1948.

❖ Met President Jimmy Carter at our military base in Ohio. I told him I was from Alabama. He stopped and said, "Where in Alabama?" I couldn't think of ONE city, because I grew up in the country!

President Carter
Bonnie and Jack (right)

❖ Tossed a coin off a Niagara Falls lookout.

❖ Ran up all the steps in front of the Philadelphia Art Museum, just as "Rocky" did in the movie!

❖ Trimmed ladies hair for 25 cents each when we lived in a Quonset Hut at the University of Colorado when Jack was in college.

❖ My voice was recognized by someone in line for a ride at Disneyworld; also, another similar incident at the Mexico City Airport!

❖ I sewed my own clothes for twenty-five years; also, I sewed many of our children's clothes as well.

❖ I led about twenty-five women's retreats out of my San Antonio home during the 1980's.

❖ I played piano for the NASA Space Center Rotary Club for seven years in Houston.

❖ A once-in-a-lifetime moment occurred when Jack and I were honored to meet Prince Philip in Buckingham Palace in 2008.

Prince Phillip   Jack and Bonnie

❖ I wore an Elvira costume for Halloween on a cruise ship, complete with wild hair and evil eye make-up. I didn't win because I didn't know how to walk like a tramp! On talent night, I played one of my favorite piano solos, "I'm in the Mood for Love." I didn't expect to ever see any of the other people again, so I went for it!

❖ I wrote and taped radio commercials for my dad's syrup business in Alabama.

❖ My first speech was to a large group of Realtors in New Jersey in 1979.

❖ When our David and Susan were preschoolers, I sewed sailor suits for them to model when our Cincinnati church sponsored a fashion show.

❖ Jack and I waved to President John Kennedy as his motorcade left the San Antonio airport the day before he was assassinated in Dallas.

❖ When my daughter, Susan, was in junior high school, she and I were testing various perfume fragrances at our favorite store. We were both about to sniff our respective bottles of perfume; instead, we looked at each other, smiled, and touched noses to sniff without thinking! This is a silly, but priceless, memory!

❖ I accidentally called General Bodycombe "General Goodbody" when he was having dinner at our home in Louisiana! He loved it but I was embarrassed!

❖ I have spit from the top of the Eiffel Tower!

❖ When visiting my Air Force brother at Nellis AFB, Las Vegas, years ago before his military retirement, he gave us a tour of his unit. He convinced me to fly the A-7 simulator (his plane at that time) and I "crashed." Then, he encouraged me to don a G-suit which the pilots must wear at high altitudes. I'll never understand how pilots can even enter a plane wearing that garb; much less attack the enemy!

❖ Another fond memory, I had worn my sister's nice pleated, plaid skirt to school one day in the ninth grade. I decided to go down the slide on the playground as we waited for the bus. Half way down the slide, the hem of that skirt was caught in one of the big screws on the slide and I was hanging on the slide half-way down! The skirt survived even though it had to be rehemmed! Not a victory but fun to remember!

❖ In the 1990's, I was about to speak to a group of church women on the personalities. En route to the sanctuary, I asked the minister's wife to wait until I made a quick stop at the restroom. I was wearing a new ensemble ~ a long silk scarf which matched my pleated skirt with a dark green corresponding sweater. As I was entering the bathroom, the long silk scarf accidentally slipped off my arm and into the commode and got wet. So, I later hung the scarf over my left arm and as I began to speak, I used that as a visual: Sanguine personalities are always getting into similar situations and it is important to quickly adapt to those situations and you'll have a much easier existence! After using my scarf as a visual, I placed in on the altar rail to dry and finished my presentation. The ladies loved it!

It is good to have your "history" in scrap books or albums in chronological order, simply to have available for projects such as above or for your family after you are gone.

I've even added below the list of famous people I have seen or met for future reference later in life when my memory "might fail":

Author Pearl Buck, Diana Krall,
Senator Margaret Chase Smith, Dr. Robert
Schuler, Dr. Billy Graham, Elvis (twice),
Debbie Reynolds, Johnny Mathis,
Robert Goulet, Jack Jones,
Rita Moreno, Delta Burke, Sandi Patti, Con-
nie Francis, Tammy Wynette, Shirley
McClain, Wyonna Judd, Frank Sinatra, Carol
Channing, Carol Lawrence, Englebert Hum-
perdink, Burt Bacharach, Ray Charles,
Mitzi Gaynor, Jim Stafford, Andy Williams,
my cousin Mel Tillis, Ethel Merman,
Claudette Colbert, Celine Dion, Rex Harrison,
Glen Campbell, the Osmonds,
many astronauts and Congressmen,
Lucie Arnez, Robert Klein, Van Johnson,
Fabio, Deana Martin, Dino, Thomas Kincade,
Yakov Smirnoff, Jim Stafford,
baseball great Jim Palmer,
Mickey Gilley, Brad Paisley,
Merlin Olden and Andy Williams.
Also, Presidents Truman, Reagan, Kennedy,
LBJ, President and Mrs. Carter
and both Presidents Bush.

RETREAT HANDOUTS

The following is an example of one of the handouts from my first women's retreat. Remember, my motivation was to encourage the ladies to think positive thoughts about themselves and to never give up, so we started at the very basics. Here are some fun suggestions of things to do to prevent boredom regardless of where you are at this time of your life whether you are speaking or simply living each day to the fullest:

WAYS TO PREVENT BOREDOM!

❖ If you get bored, go to your nearest WalMart and serve as a greeter; no one will know the difference. You can also walk around and straighten up any aisle that is untidy and no one will mind. In fact, you might share with the manager what you've done ~ he'll appreciate it.

❖ Get a cart and pick up "stray items" throughout the store and return them to their original places or simply take the cart to the manager and explain.

❖ If you see a long line at WalMart, simply get in line with a pad and pen and write down the answers to this question: "What do you like most about WalMart?" When you have about ten answers, take them to the manager and he will be delighted with your list!

❖ Work in the greeting cards section: organize and make sure each card has the correct size envelope. And, put the theme cards in correct places.

❖ Check the silk flowers and make sure they are in the correct holders. If not, organize as best as possible. Also, you might make a nice large floral arrangement, if this is one of your talents, and display it appropriately.

❖ Visit the music department: Make sure all the bins are neatly organized. If you see an operatic CD in the C & W area, find its proper space and move immediately.

❖ If you're still in WalMart and are still bored, go to the linen/bedding area and make sure all the comforters are in the correct bins and be mindful of the sizes of each item. Customers have a tendency to look, touch, move, and then discard quickly, especially if they meet a friend in that aisle. Remember there are many sizes these days ~ King, Queen, Full, Single ~ so you should allow more time, as necessary.

❖ Another area where you might be of service is at the station where film is turned in for processing. Help customers fill out that form properly and then place it in the correct area.

❖ If you have several watches in your jewelry box, it's good to take them all to WalMart and get new batteries. Enjoy wearing your watches to match an outfit ~ it's a good thing! Clean out your jewelry box and chest of drawers ~ give yourself new reasons to feel good about yourself!

TUESDAY MORNING STORES

Another store to visit is Tuesday Morning. One day I went in to my favorite local Tuesday Morning store in San Antonio to buy some of their pretty stationary and greeting cards. To my utter dismay, the entire section (stationary, note pads, all kinds of lovely cards, etc.) was a complete mess! So, I simply sat my purse down between my feet and went to work. There weren't many customers that Friday afternoon, so I spent over an hour tidying up "my aisle"!

For the next few months, I visited "my aisle" every Friday afternoon to insure things were in order. Before we moved to Oklahoma I visited my favorite store one more time and talked with Duncan, the manager. I told him what I had been doing and that he needed to find a replacement. Also, I would like a "Letter of Transfer." He said, "Bonnie, we can always tell when you've been in here and we love it! I'm sorry I can't give you a letter of transfer, but I want you to know you are always welcome to come in here and do whatever you feel is needed to enhance our store!" It takes so little to be above average!

TJ MAXX STORES

If you aren't familiar with the TJ MAXX Stores, you need to find one! Since this book is about living on a shoestring, I would be remiss if I did not share my thoughts on this store. We have a new TJ Maxx nearby and it is quite lovely. They have a good selection of journals and stationary; a fairly good selection of items for wedding gifts and many great purses for an even greater price. The quality is excellent as well. Several years ago, I found four pair of nice black slacks (tall for me which is sometimes difficult to find) on sale for only $19.99 each which I bought. They had been marked down several times and were in excellent condition. They are top of the line and I'm still wearing them after many years ~ a truly amazing buy!

As I was about to check out of our local TJ Maxx store recently, I noticed an excellent assortment of upscale cookies, high quality candies and other sweet delicacies near the checkout counters. Normally, I can talk myself out of impulse buying; however, I highly recommend the Coconut Patties! Jack and I both absolutely love these delicacies. He located the company on the web and if you cannot find a convenient TJ MAXX nearby, check out Anastasia Confections, Inc. online. I am sure they cost less at a local store, regardless, may I recommend the Coconut Patties, and I wish you luck in locating them!

SENIORS, DON'T LET AGE BE YOUR CAGE!

❖ Remember it's important to keep our minds and bodies as active and alert as possible ~ work on picture puzzles (either on the table or those on the computer) and learn to do spider solitaire on the computer if possible. Also, word puzzles are great ways to keep one's mind active. Regularly send birthday cards to all you know. You can get nice cards for a good price at Tuesday Morning!

❖ We need to have fun, laugh, and enjoy things around us.

❖ Think of ways to Bloom Where You're Planted!

❖ Remember, there's a little child within each of us and every day, we need to let that little child out to play for awhile!

❖ Don't cry because it's over ~ smile because it happened.

❖ Keep a good attitude ~ we're not here forever and we surely can't take it with us!

❖ And remember, simply going to church won't make you a Christian anymore than standing in a garage will make you a car! Get busy ~ find a cause and contribute!

❖ Don't let your worries get the best of you ~ remember, Moses started out as a basket case!

❖ We were called to be witnesses; not lawyers or judges!

❖ Ladies, do you ever feel that some days are a total waste of makeup?!

❖ When you feel least worthy ~ that's when God can use you best!

❖ Don't wait for six strong men to take you to church!

❖ Opportunity may knock once, but temptation leans on the door bell!

❖ Give God what is right ~ not what is left.

❖ Are you wrinkled with burdens? Come to the church for a face-lift!

RETIREMENT

Ladies, are you in the retirement age bracket? Life changes, doesn't it? Several things I've discovered which you may relate to on some level:

❖ I injured my left foot requiring surgery, and couldn't stand long enough to cook. And now, I think, why start back doing something I successfully stopped?!

❖ Since Jack retired, I've learned that I've been putting dishes in the washer incorrectly for 58 years! Yet, the dishes sparkled then just as they do now!

❖ We have learned to take advantage of the take out boxes at restaurants. There is plenty of food for at least three or four more meals.

❖ Don't forget to say nice things about your spouse to your children and your grandchildren.

❖ Never say, "Here I am!" Always say, "There YOU Are!" Remember, it's not about you anyway, so let it go. Life is what you make it.

❖ Continually fill your heart, soul, and mind with good, positive thoughts and, God Bless!

BROADENING YOUR HORIZONS

One of the greatest things you can do to bring happiness and joy into your life, regardless of your budget, is to broaden your horizons. Do you see any areas where you can make a change for the better? Can you think of ways in your present situation to enhance your life and those around you? Some ways that have helped me are below:

Take time to daydream and use your imagination. This is indeed a great way to enjoy life on a shoestring.

Develop new hobbies from time to time. Sooner or later we are confined to our home due to illness, age, or some other misfortune. If we have developed some good hobbies through the years, our confinement can actually be a time of becoming reacquainted with ourselves. Several years ago I had a back injury which required being sidelined for awhile. I decided I would finish reading all my half-read books, take those prescribed naps, eat properly, keep my hair neat and watch my nails grow! I played the piano when I did get up, learned several new songs, worked on jigsaw puzzles and updated my journals. What a glorious time I had. It is not often we are "ordered" to rest, but when you are confronted with any obstacle, ask yourself, "What can I learn from this?"

If you find yourself in a situation where you are babysitting several children, whether they are your own or others, why not set a schedule and turn the chore into a learning experience for the children and yourself? Organize your home and get rid of the debris. Make areas for various learning centers. Perhaps a small rug could serve as a reading, finger plays and a singing corner; another area could be a place for dolls and other toys. Don't rely on the television ~ make the day worthwhile for all. Teaching children routine, respect, manners and love is vitally important. While the schools do many of these things their jobs would be much easier if the children have a strong background based on home values.

When you read a good book, make a note of the title, author and a synopsis of the story and share this information with friends to broaden their horizons. I have a journal where I keep this information on favorite books I've read. Take your children to the library and get a library card for each child. This will encourage their reading skills. Many libraries have excellent children's programs. This can be done on a shoestring.

Regular family time is important. There's nothing to compare with a child receiving a nice warm bath at night, the smell of clean hair, a glass of milk, maybe a cookie while sitting in the lap of a parent and hearing that parent read a bedtime story! "Tucking in" children, regardless of age, is one of my most favorite memories. All children (including college students) need to be tucked in and reminded of the importance they are to your family. We all enjoy being encouraged, don't we?! I still tuck in my three when I get the chance even though all three are in their fifties!

Be alert to life! Just for fun, as you read the following football teams, see if you can think of the city each NFL group represents: BRONCOS, STEELERS, SAINTS, FALCONS, 49 'ERS, BEARS, COWBOYS,

REDSKINS, EAGLES, DOLPHINS, RAIDERS, TITANS, OILERS. And, how about these NBA teams: SPURS, MAGIC, LAKERS, HEAT, THUNDER, KNICKS, MAVER-ICKS, 76ERS, MAGIC, ROETS, KINGS, BULLS, NUG-GETS AND SUNS. This is a great way to have fun on a shoestring! I am an avid fan of the San Antonio NBA Spurs and watch every game on League Pass TV!

Devote quality time for spiritual growth. I've read "My Utmost for His Highest," daily devotional for years; I also remember reading the "Upper Room" which our church provided when in college. Listening to qual-ity music or motivational tapes while driving is yet an-other way to feed our mind with good thoughts. My friend, Carole, once told me that listening to her praise tapes while driving to and from work was the highlight of her day. Sharing memorable thoughts with others as you study scripture is a wonderful way to enhance your own spiritual life along with those whom you share.

Still other ways to fill the mind with good things in-clude traveling, inviting interesting houseguests into your home, pot luck dinners, enjoying email with friends, writing in a daily journal and studying the comments later. Also, join a book club, Toastmasters, a Bible Study group, or similar organizations. Check the week-end section of your newspaper, see what is on the com-munity calendar and check it out. Make plans to partici-pate in some of the activities. If you are single, ask friends to join you for church or some other event. The ladies in my Sunday School class enjoy monthly lunch-eons at different locations and that has been such a joy. And, always think of ways to be good to yourself! If you are good to yourself, that generosity flows out to those around you.

As a part-time travel agent several years ago, I learned about ideal vacation spots, earned a little cash, and had opportunities for an occasional trip. Many possibilities exist for individuals to earn free trips if one is willing to coordinate the details for an entire group. Along with this, I enjoy collecting travel brochures which I read later. Even if you can't afford to travel very much, reading the brochures will at least give you a preview of many locations and help you to become knowledgeable about the world in which we live.

Lastly, an excellent way to learn a great amount on any given topic, particularly in areas of the home or in travel, is to invite a group of ladies over, tell them your plan and ask each one to do research on a specific topic to be shared with the group when you meet. Each guest shares her information at the specified time followed by refreshments and discussion. There's time for learning new things, camaraderie, food and fellowship ~ true happiness on a shoestring! We can travel through the eyes of others!

20

A Thelma and Louise Trip

Can you remember who your best friends were in elementary or high school? How about the college years? Many of us have had "best friends" throughout our lives. I remember my neighbor, Mary Alice Wilkes, and often wished I had pretty blond hair as she did. And then, I remember four special friends at Crossville High School ~ Frankie Prady, Betty Tidmore, Frances Rucks and Vivian Overstreet. After moving to Jacksonville, Phyllis Rice was my best friend in high school and college. As I mentioned, we remain in touch even though we seldom see each other. It's good to have friends ~ I'm sure you have your own stories.

As I began traveling across the country speaking and participating in seminars, I have met many wonderful people. I have made a point to include in this book the importance of women needing women friends; thus, this additional chapter. As mentioned before, it's important to have friends to whom you can share your innermost thoughts or concerns, especially if you live alone. Having friends in the "golden years" gives much joy and possibly longevity to one's life. And, as an extra bonus, if we have friends near our own age whom we see often, we have less tendency to "bug" our own children who are usually busy with our grandchildren! So, friends are valuable on many levels.

It's good to be able to meet friends for coffee, lunch or dinner. Or possibly, enjoy a covered dish meal with a group where everyone brings a favorite dish to share. Some people would rather bring one dish than coordinate an entire meal. To others, it's easier to just set the table. Our church has an active senior's group which provides covered dish suppers, great programs and many scheduled trips during the year. Many churches have great programs for seniors. Whatever your likes or dislikes, it is good to have friends to occasionally join up with regardless of the reason ~ friends make the world go 'round!

I've been blessed with many friends across the country and consider them valuable enough to make efforts to stay in touch. I cherish these friends and will tell you about some of them: Florence Littauer is very dear to me on many levels ~ as a dear friend and as a mentor. I've included a picture of the two of us near the end of this book which was taken on a Christian Cruise. I've read all Florence's books and consider her one of my dearest friends. She has been a great encourager to me. There's Ann Downing in Nashville, who sponsors a fabulous women's retreat every spring called, "Middle Tennessee Women's Retreat." When you meet the ladies attending that event, you know you're meeting potential lifelong friends; Ann is also that kind of gal!

Gerry Wakeland is a very dear friend and we "bond" on many levels. She was director of Women's Ministries at the Crystal Cathedral and is now President of CLAS-Seminars, Inc., which is mentioned at the end of this book. Other friends I love and enjoy include: Julia Papageorge and Yvonne Alexander who both live in Bossier City, LA ~ Julia and I have known each other since 1976 when we lived in Bossier and were in the same church. Yvonne and I became friends through military connections. My dear friend in Nashville, Norma Spear, is such a gracious hostess and we look forward to developing a "Sisterhood" group in her area soon. I've spent several nights in her lovely home. Nancy Lodes lives in San Antonio and is my buddy who is always ready to help coordinate yet another opportunity for women to get involved and make a difference in their lives ~ we have enjoyed coordinating many programs for women together. Our friendship knows many levels! My dear friend, Gloria Sharp, and I had so much fun together when we lived in New Jersey that I devoted an entire chapter to our friendship! My special Saturday Sisters group in San Antonio will always be a part of my life and we are nearing our twentieth year of "togetherness", and still going strong. We've prayed each other through many adversities and our prayers continue. Even though I've moved to Oklahoma, I'm still part of their group. And, another group called "Sisterhood" of about ten other ladies continues to be a special part of my life as we meet occasionally across the country. Many other names come to mind: Billicarole Simmons, Pam Stephens, Gene Martin, Lou King, Barbara Morrow, Diane Roosma, all the ladies in my own extended family, Marcia Lisle, Gail Wenos, Bibby, all the MTWR ladies, and then there's Elise, my buddy! Allow me to tell you about my friend, Elise Schneider, to whom I dedicate this chapter!

I was participating in a CLASSeminar in Colorado Springs, CO, in 1989. As one of the CLASS small group leaders, my main job was to meet with the same small group each afternoon to discuss and apply what was learned on that specific day. My entire group of about twelve ladies was outstanding and a joy to lead. The attendees were excited about the new things they were learning about writing, speaking and other new horizons. And the lovely mountainous setting of our three days together added to the ambiance.

Toward the end of our last day, I learned that one of our small group members, Elise Schneider, EdD, was the President of Oxnard Community College in Oxnard, CA. She did a fabulous job with her presentations in our group. I decided it might be fun to have a college-type graduation on our last day together when the CLASS Certificates would be awarded to the attendees. I asked Elise to stand with me as I presented these certificates. She congratulated each recipient, as a college president would, with a firm handshake and adding a personal congratulations. Even though our group was small, we had a wonderful time! In fact, the group bonded so well, it was sad to see everyone leave at the end of the last afternoon for cities across the country. However, Elise and I have kept in touch since that weekend. Through the years, we have been fortunate to travel together and create even more memories.

First, our original claim to fame is that we are both Southerners - she is from Tennessee and I am from Alabama. And, we learned that we were both former Homecoming Queens, business majors in college, both have sons who are Certified Financial Planners (who have met via the phone), so we've declared ourselves "Southern Sisters"!

We made a memorable trip to Orlando, FL, from San Antonio several years ago to attend the Christian Booksellers Convention. We dubbed our trip, "The Thelma and Louise Trip," after the movie which had recently opened across the country. Elise flew to San Antonio where Jack and I lived at that time. From there, we drove east on Highway 10 from San Antonio to Orlando, FL, stopping at a Cracker Barrel for lunch one day. While there, we decided to play a game of checkers out front while taking a break. We enjoyed our trip immensely all along the way as we practiced our Southern accents! We saw a Piggly Wiggly grocery store and stopped to take pictures. We both had been away from our home states for years; however, this new bond of "Southern Sisters" allowed us the freedom of returning to our roots!

Since our children were all grown and out of college ~ we simply let our hair down and tossed our worries out the window! We enjoyed the Booksellers Convention; however, it was the trip itself that has become memorable. We discovered the joy of friendships between "mature" women as we shared our life stories with each other. I never dreamed a college president could be such fun! When I returned home Jack could not believe it when I said, "We laughed and talked all the way across the USA!" And then he added, "Well, I'm not surprised with the two of you in the car!"

Another enjoyable trip took us to Las Vegas. I flew out to CA where Elise met me at LAX and we had a delightful drive to Vegas. We had matching pajamas and agreed to bring false eyelashes for our big night in Vegas when we saw Celine Dion. Elise's eyelashes were packaged with a handy applicator but my Walmart lashes were not. I never did get my left eyelash properly lined up with my eye; however, I wore them both with pride while slightly tilting my head to offset my lousy left lash! We had such fun with those eyelashes.

To complete our drive back to her home in Port Hueneme, CA, we stopped at an older restaurant out in the desert called "Peggy Sue's 50's Restaurant" for a light lunch. And, of course, we spent some time shopping the little gift shop. Memories are made of moments such as these! We spent one night at a fabulous Bed and Breakfast and we each had a Queen Size bed where we lounged like two Reigning Queens as we enjoyed our roaring fire in the private fireplace before us! This was one of the most memorable trips of my life without Jack, who was home enjoying golf. When I returned home, he reported his golf scores and I shared with him my fun highlights with Elise.

Throughout our twenty-year friendship, Elise and I have visited each other frequently, met family and friends, talked on the phone hundreds of hours and exchanged an untold number of emails.

Once Elise was unhappy with an email she had received from Sam, her boyfriend at the time. She forwarded his email to me requesting my reaction. Because we are "sisters" at heart and very protective of one another, I shot back a scathing response evaluating each word Sam had written. I felt he should have been more caring and supportive of Elise and quite candidly elaborated in detail in the email I sent her with his original email attached.

Almost immediately I received a phone call from Elise saying she had just received a phone call from Sam saying he would really like to meet my friend, Bonnie, from whom he has just received an email!

What?? No, it couldn't be! You guessed it! I inadvertently hit "respond to all" rather than "respond to sender". Both Elise AND Sam (yikes!) had received my scathing email. How will I ever live this one down??

Years later, Elise sent me another email regarding Bob, a boyfriend she had been dating for over a year. She had accepted Bob's invitation for a two-week visit to his state to meet his family and friends. She wrote in detail their schedule of events during her upcoming visit. I appreciated her confidence in my ability to properly respond to emails by that time.

As I read Elise's email, I became so excited for her I decided I just had to immediately send her a quick response even though I was running late in departing our home to meet Jack for a special luncheon downtown. So in my typical comical, care-free manner, I responded, "I am so happy for you, Leesie, but before you go, you must agree to one thing: PROMISE ME YOU WILL NOT GET PREGNANT!"

Upon my return home, I listened to a phone message from "Leesie" that was nothing but laughter, one after another ~ absolutely no words were spoken. I thought to myself, oh my, what is this all about....what in the world could be so funny? Yes, you guessed it!! My email had been received by Elise.....AND BOB!!! Oh not again! How can "Leesie" ever forgive me for this one?? Elise called me again and said she howled in enjoyment when she received a call from Bob saying he, too, would like to meet this Bonnie-friend of hers. Fortunately, Bob had a great sense of humor about it all. I must take a moment to share with you that both Elise and Bob are relatively conservative and in their seventies! And, so am I!

Last story.....One day Elise called and asked, "Bonnie, are you sitting down?" I quickly sat down and replied, "I am now; what's up?" Elise excitedly announced that she had been invited to an event at Buckingham Palace to meet Prince Phillip. In addition, she had boldly asked if her dear friends, Colonel and Mrs. Jack Skinner, could attend as well. And the answer was an exhilarating, "yes." Thus began yet another great adventure with my buddy, Elise. The Prince, London, dinner at the Ritz Carlton, Stonehenge, and high tea at Harrods will never be the same and neither will we!!!

Friendships truly help to make the world go 'round!

Jack, Bonnie and Elise
Enjoying a cobbler at Branson

21

Reaching Out to Others on a Shoestring

The following ideas are provided as examples of ways to encourage others to live a more meaningful life regardless of one's budget:

DECLUTTER AUCTION:

January is a great month to have a Declutter Auction. This is a time when we are cleaning up after the holidays and chances are, we have some items we do not need anymore. Our church ladies enjoy event this every January. Each person brings one item from her home that she no longer wants or needs (no bought items). All items are placed on the dining table for "viewing" prior to the auction. It is good to let the ladies peruse the items beforehand to increase enthusiasm.

A covered dish luncheon may be a good idea for your group. I serve a simple buffet meal using disposable plates, napkins, and flatware which are quickly cleaned up. My favorite meal to serve is a sandwich ring from SAM's Club, which feeds about twenty. The ring can be cut into individual serving sizes and left in the original container to serve. Add chips, a cookie and a drink and not only is this delicious but easily cleaned up afterwards.

Since our dining room table is covered with the donated items for bidding, I set up snack trays and let the ladies sit on the stairs or patio ~ wherever they can find a place ~ this adds to the informal festivities. Keep the excitement focused on the bidding! Encourage everyone to help tidy up in anticipation of the auction.

Next, pass out a predetermined amount of play money (I use $410 for psychological reasons!) to each person. The amount of money I chose is for this reason: Four hundred dollars is impressive and the extra $10 makes it even more exciting. It's not nearly $500, but it's an amount where it is wise to think twice before spending. And, if you have a larger sum, the auction will take too long...........but, use whatever amount you feel acceptable. It is wise to invite all the ladies to count their money again to make sure they have the correct amount. This encourages them to "claim" the money in a fun way which also adds to the excitement!

Every January, I host two or three of these events in my own home, or churches for various groups. The key is to have a fun loving sanguine personality as the auctioneer. Display items to be auctioned on a table which is visible to all. This is a perfect thing to do on a shoestring. The play money may be obtained at a Party City store or similar store. The original idea for these auctions came from SweetMonday.org and I encourage you to check that address out!

Afterthoughts: Years ago our church held "box suppers" which were fun. The young ladies of the church decorated shoe boxes with various décor and then add food. The night of the event, the auctioneer did a great job of "selling" all the boxes to the young men in the audience. The person with the highest bid on each box earned the right to eat the contents with the owner! This was a money making event for our church. It is good to share memories such as this. Perhaps someone in your group has similar memories they would enjoy sharing.

BABY SITTING CO-OP:

When our children were still quite young, Jack and I often enjoyed seeing a movie or playing bridge with friends. Since we were all living on a shoestring during that time, we had to watch our pennies. A Baby Sitting Co-op was founded and from then on we had no baby sitting expenses. This is how it worked:

We used the point system: For each fifteen minutes we sat for someone else, we earned one point; hence, we earned four points for an hour. The moms alternated acting as bookkeeper, keeping the records and coordinating any baby sitting jobs. When we baby sat in other member's home, we earned points. So, the bookkeeper kept an account of all activity. This is a great way to ensure the wellbeing of your children while at the same time having a "free" evening to spend with others.

FRIENDSHIP COFFEES:

This takes a bit of responsibility on the part of the hostess but I did the following for several years and felt as blessed as those attending. This is for someone who might enjoy hosting a coffee at the same time each month in their home. The idea is to provide a meeting place so your friends and neighbors will know that's a great day for visiting and enjoying each other every month. I chose the last Monday of the month, from ten until twelve noon. We called our gatherings "Friendship Coffees." The first few gatherings were just coffee, tea and a pastry of some kind. Our group bonded so beautifully, I thought it might be nice to have a very short devotional and some kind of simple program (to make the morning worthwhile). For the devotional, I simply selected a Bible verse that meant something to me and added a few remarks and a prayer.

Our "simple" programs evolved into bigger programs and we had an amazing time over the next three years! Several ladies volunteered to give book reports on their favorite books; another gave a presentation on "Dressed for Success" while yet another spoke on "Parenting", and one lady who was a hairdresser, gave a great presentation on care of the hair, etc. We had a fabulous array of programs given by the ladies themselves! Many of the ladies had never done such a thing. This was a great opportunity for them to grow as individuals while sharing their interests with others. Also, there are people who are always pleased to come free of charge to give demonstrations or presentations on various subjects. It takes so little to be above average!

SUNSHINE CLUB:

In the 1960's, we lived in Clear Lake City, Texas, next to NASA. Our new church was growing in every possible way; however, there was not yet a program for the seniors.

This was years ago before the seniors were going to Branson on a regular basis! I invited the ladies to my home for coffee and when a roomful of ladies made their appearance, I knew something should be done immediately to provide more activities for these sweet ladies.

Following a time of getting acquainted, we discussed the future of this group. We scheduled a monthly coffee at my home, the ladies wanted to alternate bringing the pastries and the following gatherings featured short programs as well. We decided to get a name for our group and that in itself was fun ~ no one wanted the word, "Seniors", mentioned! We eventually decided on the "Sunshine Club" and this little group proved "it takes so little to be above average"! One month we had coffee, a short Bible study and then played various games from our childhood. Each month was more creative than the last ~ seniors have a wealth of talent just waiting to be exploited.

This is a great opportunity for someone looking to serve in a church situation ~ open your home and heart and they do the rest!

THEME COFFEES OR LUNCHEONS:

This event will cost <u>you</u> the price of a meal, but it's a great investment. There are many themes you may dream up on your own and your friends may surprise you with even more ideas.

My dear friend, Nancy Lodes, and I enjoyed the most memorable "Victorian Luncheon" at a San Antonio restaurant which featured beautiful décor of the Victorian era. We thought it would be fun to invite other ladies interested in that era to join us in creating Victorian ensembles for ourselves for the occasion! I found a gorgeous off-white long chiffon Victorian-looking gown for only $10 at a resale shop and it fit perfectly. At another resale shop I found a wide brim floppy off-white hat which worked well with my gown. The other ladies had a grand time assembling their Victorian outfits as well and we had a lovely luncheon. The restaurant manager gladly reserved the choice table in his restaurant for us and I truly believe he enjoyed our meal as much as we did! While we were finishing our desserts, each person shared a short story on some aspect of the Victorian Era which was of interest to her or anything she would like to share. We took pictures afterwards and the other customers enjoyed our outing as well!

We enjoyed the Victorian luncheon so much that we planned a lovely Victorian Holiday Tea at our church. My friend, Nancy, and I also co-hosted this event and it was magical. We decorated round tables with Victorian settings using vintage Santas as centerpieces. We played lovely music from that era, invited other ladies to help with refreshments, served tea from beautiful china and had a memorable event. It was thrilling to see what the ladies created for their apparel for the tea, especially the hats! If you have some local musicians who could provide background classical music, or perhaps simply play CDs, it is thrilling to simply walk around and enjoy the ambiance! We also co-hosted another Victorian Tea at the "Commander's House" in San

Antonio, a Victorian home which provided a perfect location downtown for an amazing event. Invite others to help you plan and decorate. You will be amazed at the contributions others make when least suspected. This is a great opportunity to live vicariously through others and become familiar with some customs of a past era.

Nancy is one of the most gracious people I know and one of my dearest friends. This picture was taken on her back patio. Those in the photo are Bonnie, Nancy, Linda & Blye (from top to bottom).

SATURDAY SISTERS:

Almost twenty years ago, a group of ladies in our Sunday School Class in San Antonio were invited to a luncheon at the home of Lee Wilkins in our class, primarily to become better acquainted. Lee served a lovely luncheon and as we were about to leave that day, one of the ladies asked if we might pray for a particular situation that was happening in her family. And then, another asked for prayer as well. These concerns were remembered and one of the other ladies invited us to her home the following month for another luncheon. There were more prayer requests and some prayer updates from the first gathering and we had a wonderful time.

And now after all these years, the group continues to meet monthly. We have prayer journals, and are truly wonderful friends forever. There's nothing we would not do for each other! When it is our turn to be hostess, we serve lovely meals because we want our "sisters" to have the best! We use our "best dishes" not to impress but to show that we truly love each other and have great concern for all our family members. We are truly "Sisters in Christ"! And now that we are becoming "seniors," we also share our health and family concerns. It is good to have such a wonderful group to share unconditional love and to know there is always someone to call if we have a need of any kind. When we moved to Oklahoma, about six years ago, I was sorry to leave my group of "Sisters" but, they wouldn't "release" me from the group, so I continue to attend events when possible; also, I get updates on everyone by email and feel just as much a part of the group as always being there in person. If you feel you would like to start your own group such as this, I encourage you to do so.

Invite a few ladies over and discuss the possibilities of getting together and making a difference in your lives ~ you'll be glad you did!

IMPORTANCE OF BFF's (BEST FRIENDS FOREVER)

If you have lonely days, feeling sad, wishing there was someone nearby to simply share a cup of coffee with, or you desperately need someone you could talk with who might encourage you, this is for YOU! Whether you're a stay-at-home-mom, a senior mom or a working mom, your life is no-doubt hectic and there's little time to enjoy friendships with others in your similar situation. Perhaps your children have "flown the coop" and you may even have grandchildren, or, it may be that you are finally at home, retired, from a position that has left you wondering, "Is this all there is to life?"

Blye, Linda, Kathy, Betty Claire, Nancy
(front row) Cindy, "Lee", Billicarole & Bonnie

Regardless of your situation in life at this time, it is a well known fact that women need women friends. We like to talk things through, we like to discuss, we like to hear both sides of a story, we like to encourage, and we like to be encouraged when we're depressed.

We like to discuss shopping, hobbies, sorrows, woes, travel, family concerns and also concerns when we become widows. We need the sisterhood to keep us balanced. What are some ways to foster female friendships? The following may be of help to you; also, think of other ways you might find to foster these normal feelings mentioned above.

WOMEN NEED WOMEN FRIENDS!

❖ Select one or two other ladies you feel share your interests.

❖ Have a Friendship Coffee for your contacts and offer it monthly. Have a simple program where others may help ~ don't do it all yourself!

❖ Organize a pot luck luncheon or dinner and invite ladies you feel would be interested in becoming better acquainted ~ not to impress each other but to sincerely love one another and encourage; perhaps make future plans for friendship. Have programs, travel or simply have fun! Again, follow up! Above all, be an encourager! Don't do all the work yourself ~ ask others to share their talents and help and they will.

❖ Join a Bible Study, Gym or Exercise Class. Get names and phone numbers and call them later. Keeping in touch is the key to building lasting relationships and groups.

❖ If you are a senior, find a church with a great Senior's Program which includes traveling throughout the years. The motor coaches traveling to Branson are geared to care for seniors ~ and they drop you off at the front entrance to all theatres! Plus, there's so much fun on those motor coaches and all the people are friendly ~ it's a worry-free trip!

❖ Check out alumni events from your high school and/or college. Contact old friends. You'll learn you are not the only one aging!

❖ Invite those women to a coffee and makes some plans. Follow up.

❖ Join or create a baby sitting co-op as I previously mentioned.

❖ Form a Planning Committee and enlist other ladies you meet. Have a goal to enjoy life. Don't let age be your cage ~ celebrate life!

❖ If your church has a women's organization of any kind, you might volunteer in some area and make a difference in all you do.

❖ Read some of Florence Littauer's books on the personalities and Dr. Kevin Leman's books on "The Birth Order" ~ and have discussions. These subjects will change your life!

SISTERHOOD FRIENDS:

Nancy Lodes is one of my dearest friends. She is fun, gracious, kind, a Godly woman and very active in her San Antonio Church. We have enjoyed working on various projects together through the years. We look forward to meeting in various homes, maybe enjoying a holiday dinner cruise on one of the barges that travels around the downtown scenic San Antonio River. It is always great to see the tall cypress trees along the river banks decorated with the long strings of Christmas lights reflecting in the water. Most of all, it is great to be with dear friends once again. Now, that's what "Happiness On a Shoestring!" is all about!

And finally, when you see an article that makes you feel good in some way, I encourage you to post it on your bulletin board or the fridge or wherever you can easily read from time to time; also, share with others. Keep feeding your mind with positive things regardless of your age. And, share these thoughts with others.

Here are some more thoughts that I enjoy referring to often:

❖ I believe that it isn't always enough to be for-given by others. Sometimes you have to learn to forgive yourself.

❖ I believe that no matter how bad your heart is broken, the world doesn't stop for your grief.

❖ I believe that our background and circum-stances may have influenced who we are, but we are responsible for who we become.

❖ I believe that you shouldn't be so eager to find out a secret. It could change your life forever.

❖ I believe two people can look at the exact same thing and see something totally differ-ent. As my son says, "Learn to disengage!"

❖ I believe that your life can be changed in a matter of hours by people who don't even know you.

❖ I believe that the people you care about most in life are often taken from you too soon.

❖ I believe that even when you think you have no more to give, if a friend cries out to you........you will find the strength to help.

❖ I believe that credentials on the wall do not make you a decent human being. What you feel in your heart is what truly counts.

❖ The happiest of people don't necessarily have the best of everything; they simply ~

MAKE THE MOST OF EVERYTHING!

22

What I've Learned

❖ The importance of setting short and long-term goals; and the value of continually updating.

❖ The significance of executing and carrying out those goals ~ don't just put "things" on paper.

❖ Keep the weeds out of your life (things that "pull" you down).

❖ Claim a Bible Verse to lead the way (my favorite has always been Matthew 6:33). *"Seek ye first, the Kingdom of God, and all these things shall be added unto you."*

❖ Realize the importance of reaching out to others; learn to ask good questions, and, then follow up with another good question.

This is the key to making others happy and brings joy to yourself!

❖ Have at least one success every day, whether big or small.

❖ Realize that you can make a difference regardless of your current situation. Set a good example wherever you are.

❖ Keep personal belongings in order so you'll have an orderly life.

❖ Hold friends dear and near; be creative and make plans to do this.

❖ Strive to live an exemplary life in all ways ~ and know that this takes study and effort.

❖ Never forget: others are watching YOU.

❖ Go to bed with a clean face always, free of makeup (maybe night cream :)

❖ Be good to yourself and others will be good to you!

❖ Know what you want out of life; continue your education in all ways possible ~ attending classes, reading and sharing are all excellent ways to do that. Be alert to events happening in your area. Get a group together and attend functions.

❖ Once you achieve one goal, make another one and keep positive as you go. Don't rest on your laurels.

❖ Keep short and long-term goals updated to offset failures along the way.

❖ Maintain a thankful attitude. Remember, you don't always have to be in charge! Encourage others to grow and let them lead as well.

❖ Again, never underestimate the value of asking good, leading questions; also, follow-up questions are just as important ~ that's the joy of encouraging others. This bears repeating over and over.

❖ Give to the world the best you have and the best will come back to you!

❖ Stay humble and be appreciative of what God has given you.

AND SO.......

If you can't be a highway,

Then just be a trail

If you can't be the moon, be a star

It isn't by size that you win or you fail ~

Be the BEST of whatever you are!

~ Douglas Malloch

ADDITIONAL PHOTOS

Family and Friends

Our Family - David, Susan, Becky, Bonnie and Jack

Crossvile Reunion of
Friends:
Tommie, Frankie,
Betty, Bonnie
and Frances

ADDITIONAL PHOTOS

Family and Friends

Bonnie and
Florence Littauer

Bonnie and Jack

To Schedule the Author for Speaking Engagements and Ordering Books

Contact: Bonnie Skinner
623 36th Avenue, NW
Norman, OK 73072-4106
Email: b.skinner@cox.net

Additional Information

Christian Leaders Authors and Speakers Seminars (CLASS)

Noted Christian Speaker and Author of numerous books, Florence Littauer, is the founder of CLASS. For additional information regarding this important seminar plus additional programs to help you achieve your highest potential, the following information is offered:

Gerry Wakeland, President, CLASSEMINARS, Inc.
(CLASSEMINARS.org)
P.O. Box 36551
702-882-0638
Albuquerque NM 87176

I was honored to be a member of Florence Littauer's CLASS Staff for several years, traveling across the United States presenting this great seminar to groups. If you are interested in enhancing your writing, speaking, and communication skills, CLASS is for YOU! Contact Gerry Wakeland (above) for more details.

* * * * * * * * * * * * * * * *

Middle Tennessee Women's Retreat (MTWR)

Another event I'm sure you will enjoy is the annual Middle Tennessee Women's Retreat in Nashville, affectionately known as "MTWR," founded by Gospel Singer, Ann Downing. Every spring women from over twenty states attend this three-day retreat. As a member of the staff, I'd love to see you there! Bring a group from your church or area ~ Great Music & Program!

For More Details: Call Ann Downing at 615-822-1900